Cambridge E

C000246598

Elements in Gender
edited by
Tiffany D. Barnes
University of Kentucky
Diana Z. O'Brien
Washington University in St. Louis

IN LOVE AND AT WAR

Marriage in Non-state Armed Groups

Hilary Matfess
*University of Denver's Josef Korbel School
of International Studies*

Shaftesbury Road, Cambridge CB2 8EA, United Kingdom

One Liberty Plaza, 20th Floor, New York, NY 10006, USA

477 Williamstown Road, Port Melbourne, VIC 3207, Australia

314–321, 3rd Floor, Plot 3, Splendor Forum, Jasola District Centre, New Delhi – 110025, India

103 Penang Road, #05–06/07, Visioncrest Commercial, Singapore 238467

Cambridge University Press is part of Cambridge University Press & Assessment, a department of the University of Cambridge.

We share the University's mission to contribute to society through the pursuit of education, learning and research at the highest international levels of excellence.

www.cambridge.org
Information on this title: www.cambridge.org/9781009486019

DOI: 10.1017/9781009358859

First published 2024

A catalogue record for this publication is available from the British Library

ISBN 978-1-009-48601-9 Hardback
ISBN 978-1-009-35889-7 Paperback
ISSN 2753-8117 (online)
ISSN 2753-8109 (print)

In Love and at War

Marriage in Non-state Armed Groups

Elements in Gender and Politics

DOI: 10.1017/9781009358859
First published online: January 2024

Hilary Matfess
University of Denver's Josef Korbel School of International Studies
Author for correspondence: Hilary Matfess, hilary.matfess@gmail.com

Abstract: What does it mean to be in love while at war? This Element demonstrates that whether rebel groups commit themselves to marriage, bar it entirely, or reinterpret the ceremonies and practices associated with marriage, their decision has important implications for both the rebel organization and individual members. This Element contributes to the literature on gender and politics by demonstrating that rebel marriages are an underappreciated driver of gendered conflict and post-conflict dynamics. It introduces frameworks for understanding how rebel groups approach the issue of marriage, suggesting that variation between and within rebel groups over time is related to not only the rebels' political project but also the anticipated effect of marriage on cohesion and retention, as well as the rebels' logistical concerns. Furthermore, the Element unpacks how wartime rebel marriages can complicate or improve women's prospects for post-conflict reintegration by shaping whether rebel wives are depoliticized, distrusted, or reclaimed.

Keywords: gender, marriage, post-conflict reintegration, female rebels, non-state armed groups

ISBNs: 9781009486019 (HB), 9781009358897 (PB), 9781009358859 (OC)
ISSNs: 2753-8117 (online), 2753-8109 (print)

Contents

Preface

Listening to Mariam[1] and Fikru's[2] love story while sitting around their kitchen table in Addis Ababa, Ethiopia's capital city, I was reminded of all the times before that I have heard happily and long-wed couples describe how they met. There is a degree of mythmaking and a rhythm to their back-and-forth. At times I felt like an audience member taking in a well-rehearsed play; captivated, I watched Mariam and Fikru recite familiar lines to their latest audience. His eyes sparkled and he looked at her with clear and genuine adoration as he described to me the promises that he made to her during their wartime courtship as members of the Tigray People's Liberation Front (TPLF) and his predictions of what their life together would be like after victory. She, pragmatic and witty as ever, parried his romanticism, while clearly relishing her role as the object of his affection.

While their repartee and obvious affection for one another reminded me of many married couples, I grasped the exceptional nature of their relationship when I toured the Martyrs' Memorial Museum in Mekelle, Tigray. The museum is dedicated to documenting the TPLF's fight against the military dictatorship, a struggle that stretched from the mid-1970s to 1991, when a coalition of rebel groups led by the TPLF marched into Addis Ababa. As I wandered through an exhibit of photos of the rebels during the war, I suddenly found myself in front of a large portrait of Mariam and Fikru. In the photo, they are side by side, with his arm around her, beaming. Their faces were smoother and their hair darker, but they were instantly recognizable. From our conversation, I knew they fell in love during the war, but seeing this photo in a museum dedicated to the heroes of the struggle gave a new sense of importance and historical weight to their story. I snapped a photo of the portrait with my cellphone, so that I could share it with Mariam later. As I continued to meander through the exhibit hall, I thought about how incredible it was that their dedication to one another had persisted through the war, the transitional period, party schisms, several decades of TPLF rule, and parenthood. I thought about what it meant to be in love while at war.

That spontaneous conversation at a kitchen table in Addis Ababa sparked an interest in how marriage shapes rebels' experiences during and after war – and convinced me that a thorough examination of rebels' marriage practices can provide us with a more holistic understanding of how rebel groups operate, the dynamics of women's contributions to rebellion, and the contours of women's lives after war. So many of the discussions about marriage in war that I encountered early in this project focused on forced marriage and centered experiences of coercion, abuse, and sexual violence. While these are important

---

[1] A pseudonym (which also means 'Beloved' in Tigrinya).

[2] A pseudonym (which also means 'His Love' in Tigrinya).

experiences to document and understand, these accounts did not capture the experiences of Mariam and Fikru, for whom marriage was a source of comfort and affection, during and after war.

While this Element is an academic attempt to position women's lives and feminine subjects like marriage seriously in the study of political violence, it would border on dishonesty to ignore the ways in which this project is informed by my own experience of getting married just one week after I submitted my dissertation.[3] Getting married meant navigating formal requirements imposed by the state and informal expectations levied by family and friends. Sorting through the traditions and norms associated with marriage to decide what suits me and my partner is an exhausting, illuminating, and ongoing process; as someone who identifies as a feminist, it can feel like walking on eggshells through a minefield.[4]

Though the insecurity and militarization that characterize rebel marriages are not present in most civilian marriages (including my own), the institution of marriage itself carries with it questions about gender roles and norms and, in the case of heterosexual marriage in particular, women's role in society. As much as we might like to think of the home as a refuge from politics, the relationships, expectations, and routines that we experience in the home *are* deeply political. As Celello and Kholoussy (2016) note, "Marriage frequently becomes a vehicle for critiquing larger socioeconomic and political changes, for shaping public policy and for endeavoring to eradicate perceived social ills" (p. 2). The truism that 'the personal is political' remains relevant in rebel groups and times of war.

Introduction

At face value, love and war seem to be incongruous areas of study, tethered most famously by the aphorism that all is fair under both conditions. Yet, just as there are laws of war, the ways in which love is practiced are also subject to regulation. Marriage is perhaps the most universal and durable way in which love has been institutionalized and regulated. Fineman (2001) is worth quoting at length regarding how marriage has significance for both the spouses it binds and society writ large; she writes:

> Marriage can be experienced as: a legal tie, a symbol of commitment, a privileged sexual affiliation, a relationship of hierarchy and subordination, a means of self-fulfillment, a societal construct, a cultural phenomenon,

---

[3] It was a joyful and exhausting week that I am happy is now in the rearview mirror.

[4] I grappled, for example, with the question of whether to have my father walk me down the aisle. I was not keen on the connotations of property transfer that it seemed to imply, but my father is my best friend and I wanted to honor our bond. In the end, I decided to have my father walk me down the aisle and we laughed the whole way.

a religious mandate, an economic relationship, a preferred reproductive unit, a way to ensure against poverty and dependency, a romantic ideal, a natural or divined connection, a stand-in for morality, a status, or a contractual relationship. (p. 239)

Fineman (2001) goes on to unpack the implications that marriage has for the community writ large, noting that:

> From the state's perspective, marriage may mean the imposition of order necessary for record-keeping purposes (e.g., to facilitate property transfers at death) . . . It has been argued that marriage is the preferred method of containing and harnessing [male] sexuality in the interests of the larger society. Marriage can reflect the moral or religious convention of a society – a symbolic function. Marriage can also be the site where essential reproductive tasks are preformed for society . . . Finally, marriage can be the mechanism through which society distributes and delivers social goods to its citizens. (p. 239)

Thus, marriage, whether governed by the terms of the state, colonial governments, religious or traditional authorities, or non-state armed groups, is an institution between individuals that reflects broader power dynamics and whose implications reverberate beyond the household. Exercising influence over who can be married and under what conditions is thus a powerful authority – and contestation may arise over who can legitimately claim jurisdiction over marital regulations and proceedings.

In conflict-affected contexts, controlling marriage can be another way in which rebels assert their legitimacy vis-à-vis the existing authorities – whether religious, political, or social. Rebel groups' approaches to marriage underline that the institution is a "part of the symbolic struggle between rebels and incumbents in the realm of morality, under the critical gaze of broader society" (Gayer, 2013: 357). Rebels' marriage policies are thus a way in which the politics of the home have implications for the rebels' broader campaign.

This Element demonstrates that whether rebels wed themselves to the idea of marriage, bar it entirely, or reinterpret the ceremonies and practices associated with marriage, their decision has implications at both the organizational and the individual levels. At the organizational level, marriage regulations affect recruitment, retention, logistical capabilities, and relations with the civilian population. At the individual level, a rebel organization's approach to marriage shapes how women join the organization, their experiences as members, and their post-conflict economic and social prospects. Furthermore, I consider the ways in which marriages in rebel groups – whether coerced or voluntary – can become the site of affection, care, and even love among spouses (Matfess, in press).

This Element contributes to the literature on gender and politics in four key ways. Firstly, it provides an analytical framework (the Strategies and Tactics of

Rebel Marriage, or STORM) for understanding how and why rebel marriage systems vary between and within groups over time, as well as the implications of these changes for women's lives. I suggest that the relationship between traditional heterosexual marriage dynamics and the rebels' broader political project, the anticipated effect of marriage on rebel cohesion and retention, and whether marriage will be considered a boon or drain on rebels' resources and logistical capabilities determine the rebels' approach to marriage. I use accounts from five different rebel groups, TPLF in Ethiopia, the Communist Party of Nepal – Maoists (CPN-M), the Liberation Tigers of Tamil Eelam (LTTE) in Sri Lanka, al-Shabaab in Kenya and Somalia, and the Islamic State in Iraq and Syria, to underscore the utility of this framework for explaining differences in policies towards marriage between rebel groups and within the same group over time.

Secondly, I also introduce the concept of 'the other DDR', which can emerge alongside the disarmament, demobilization, and reintegration (DDR) programs in the postwar period, intended to smooth former combatants' transition to civilian life. 'The other DDR' refers to the narratives of depoliticization, distrust, and reclamation (DDR) that emerge in response to rebel marriages and rebel wives after war. I detail how these narratives affect women's experiences and opportunities after war. In providing these frameworks, I contribute to the literature on rebel group dynamics and the burgeoning literature on women's lives within rebel groups and after war. I unpack how the STORM framework can help us understand how wartime practices and identities will shape the manifestation of this 'other DDR'. In so doing, I connect the decisions made at the organizational level to the individual experiences of women after war.

Thirdly, this Element furthers the call to consider the dynamics of "love and care" that emerge during times of war (Krystalli and Schulz, 2022; Manivannan et al., 2023).[5] Much of the research on marriage in rebel groups centers on understanding instances of forced marriage (Donnelly and Myers, 2023). Recent research, for example, has sought to differentiate between forced marriage and sexual slavery; such work emphasizes the myriad nonsexual functions of marriage but still centers coercion and violence as a central aspect of rebel marriage systems.[6] In this Element, I further Giri's assertion

---

[5] A point also raised by Giri, K. (2023). Rebel Governance of Marriage and Sexuality: An Intersectional Approach. International Studies Quarterly, 67(2). https://doi.org/10.1093/isq/sqad028.
[6] The authors note that

> What distinguishes the two is that in forced marriage, the nonstate armed group deems the forced relationship a marriage, deems its participants spouses, or officiates the relationship with a marital ceremony or documentation. This distinction between forced marriage and sexual slavery is not just semantic. While survivors of forced marriage are likely to have been forced to perform sexual acts, and survivors of sexual

that "to gain a more nuanced understanding of the complex interplay between marriage and sexuality and rebel governance, we need to go beyond violence/ coercion ... Hence, the study of marriage and sexuality in rebel governance should not only examine remunerative and coercive aspects but also include noncoercive normative structures and practices".[7] Without underplaying the extent to which rebel marriages can be a form of violence and may be arranged and enforced through tremendous coercion, we must also recognize the ways in which these unions can be arenas of "love and care" (Krystalli and Schulz, 2022).

At the organizational level, "as a forum for horizontal socialization, marriage among rebels can spur renewed devotion to the organization and its cause or detract from revolutionary zeal; it may represent an actualization of rebel ideology or an uncomfortable compromise between ideology and practicality" (Matfess, in press). As previously discussed, rebel marriage can also be a symbolic feature of the rebels' struggle against the prevailing authorities. At the individual level, rebel spouses can become a source of comfort and affection, helping one another to weather the trials of conflict and to understand their place in the rebellion. Marriages among rebels can be, at once, the site of profound harm and sincere affection for the spouses involved.

Fourthly and relatedly, this Element is inspired by feminist scholars' efforts to take seriously women's lives and experiences, to question why 'feminine' subjects have been relegated to the margins of security studies, to consider how love and joy still manifest in times of war (Krystalli and Schulz, 2022), and to demonstrate how more inclusive approaches can provide a better understanding of conflict and post-conflict dynamics (Donnelly, 2018). As Cynthia Enloe, a foundational thinker in the field of feminist security studies, once stated:

> To be doing feminist work everyday, to live like a feminist, you have to take women's lives seriously. It doesn't mean that you have to think that every woman is an angel or every woman is politically astute – that is not what feminists believe. They believe that you have got to take all kinds of women seriously or you'll never understand women's relationships to men, men's relationships to each other, or men's relationships to different forms of activism and to governments. (quoted in Van Hook, 2012)

---

slavery might have been forced to perform "wifely" duties, forced marriage encompasses more than a sexual relationship. (Donnelly and Myers, 2023)

[7] See also Loken (in press) on the relationship between women's participation in rebel groups and rebel governance.

As such, we do not have to see ourselves in these rebel women or their marriages for them to be an important wartime dynamic that merits attention from academics and policymakers.

In sum, the Element provides a lens to understand marriages among rebels beyond the instances in which these unions are a form of sexual violence and coercion. Additionally, it offers a better understanding of the sources of variation in rebels' policies on marriage both between and within rebel groups. Furthermore, it provides a framework to understand the connections between organizational decisions about marriage in rebel groups and the experiences of individual rebels during and after war. Throughout, I endeavor to center women's experiences and to underscore what is lost when we marginalize 'feminized' subjects in the study of war.

Before delving into the heart of this Element, a few points regarding terminology and project motivation are necessary. It is important to recognize that many of the unions that I discuss are instances of forced marriage, in which one or both of the partners is not in a position to refuse the arrangement.[8] In some academic studies of forced marriage, the authors use quotation marks to discuss such arrangements (i.e. stylizing it as 'marriage') (see Denov and Drumbl, 2020). I have not adopted that convention in this Element for both substantive and stylistic reasons. Without undermining the grave human rights violation that forced marriages constitute, it is important to recognize that these unions can be regarded as being 'legitimate' marriages by the husband, the wife, and other members of the community. Reflecting on a marriage between an abducted woman and an officer (Amito and Onen, respectively) that began as a forced marriage within the Lord's Resistance Army (LRA), Dubal noted that "if Amito and Onen's marriage had indeed been a 'crime against humanity,' it was not a crime that Amito or either of their families cared to recognise given how it had developed over time" (Dubal, 2016: 28). Similarly, 80 percent of the individuals subjected to forced marriage by the Khmer Rouge in Cambodia regarded their marriages as legitimate, according to interviews conducted by LeVine (2010).[9] Her account also underscores the linguistic differentiation her respondents made when describing their experiences under the Khmer Rouge; she writes: "in the context of that time, respondents used the word 'forced' to describe work conditions, no one used the same word to describe their marriages" (LeVine, 2010: 175). Hers and other research suggest that people (including women) can exercise limited agency under conditions of forced

---

[8] For a history on the rise of forced marriage as a crime under international law, see Bunting, Tasker, and Lockhart (2021).

[9] LeVine's (2010) study also notes a perhaps surprising degree of continuity in these relationships, even after the fall of the Khmer Rouge.

marriage and that affection can develop even in the context of a forced marriage (see Bunting, Tasker, and Lockhart, 2021).[10] Pinpointing the moment at which a forced marriage becomes a union that both husband and wife want to maintain, moving their relationship from a 'marriage' to a marriage, is a near impossible task in the context of this Element.

The Element proceeds as follows. In the following section, I briefly summarize the academic literature on marriage in war, considering what can be gleaned from the study of military marriage and describing the threads of commonality that emerge from the extant literature on the dynamics of rebel marriage at the organizational and individual levels. The next section introduces the STORM framework to understand variation in how non-state armed groups approach marriage during war and why rebels change their approach over time. I then connect the STORM framework to the study of former rebel women's lives, discussing how the forms of rebel marriage practiced influence which of the narratives in 'the other DDR' may be most prevalent. In so doing, I illustrate the legacies of rebel marriage, particularly for women. The final section summarizes the arguments in this Element and discusses areas for future research on non-state armed groups' approach to marriage and the legacies of these unions.

Marriage in War: A Crisis? A Complement? A Conundrum

> After all, what is messier than marriage? And who on the world stage is more trivial – worthy of trivialization – than a mere wife?
>
> (Enloe, 2016: 321)

As discussed in the Introduction, marriage has implications for the individuals involved in the union, the organizations that are responsible for regulating and sanctifying these unions, as well as society writ large. These functions are just as relevant in times of war as in times of peace. In the first part of this section, I briefly review the literature on how state-affiliated militaries have grappled with marriage in their ranks. In doing so, I draw out the implications of wartime marriage for the military as an organization and for women's lives during and after war. I use this discussion to contextualize and motivate

---

[10] Bunting, Tasker, and Lockhart (2021) write:

> The small rebels were considered unable to provide the same protection as commanders or higher-ranking soldiers, and therefore were less preferred by women, even in these confined circumstances. This is captured by the following quote: "One of the rebels, a lower ranked asked me that he wanted me to come and live with him just like a wife and a husband, I told him that no, I do not want to be his wife because he was also a new abductees and with lower rank, I thought this would create problems between the commanders because he had not lived there for long just like me" (Interview 2, Uganda). (p. 624)

a deeper study of rebel marriage. Though there are myriad differences between state and non-state armed groups, Enloe notes that there are surprising commonalities between how these two types of armed groups integrate women; she writes that though "the ideological rationales behind women's recruitment in liberation armies are indeed different from statist rationales, actual practices of liberation militaries and state militaries frequently look strikingly similar" (Enloe, 1980: 49). Thus, we can anticipate some degree of similarity between militaries' and rebels' concern with the management of marriage and the implications it has for women in the organization.

In the second part of the section, I draw out the literature on rebel marriages specifically, synthesizing and summarizing the state of scholarship on the subject. In line with the scope conditions of this Element, I consider the relevance of marriage both for rebel organizations and for the individual wives in these marriages.[11] In doing so, I highlight the contributions of this Element to this burgeoning – but often siloed – area of study.

What It Means to Make a Military Man: Masculinity and Marriage in the Armed Forces

Many militaries have explicitly or implicitly benefited from the connections between military service, masculinity, and marriageability. Writing on the British military in the 1700s, Hurl-Eamon observes that soldiers could be enticed both by the military's reputation for swashbuckling womanizing (noting "the words of an early nineteenth-century ballad refrain: 'storm the trenches court the wenches'" expressed "key elements of the soldiering life") and because marriage may have been easier as a soldier than as an apprentice (Hurl-Eamon, 2014: 105). Such associations between access to women and military service remain relevant hundreds of years later. Reflecting on Bolivia, Gill writes that men serve "to earn respect from women (mothers, wives, sisters, and girlfriends) and male peers, both as defenders of the nation and, more broadly, as strong, responsible male citizens who can make decisions and lead" (Gill, 1997: 527). Similarly, one American veteran recalled:

> Like so many other veterans, I joined the military at least in part to get girls – something my recruiter, drill instructors, and all of 1980s American popular culture assured me was a wise investment of my time and energy. The contract I signed had explicit terms of service, but it also contained an implicit cultural codicil: those who use violence to defend the nation receive something special in return – a manly prestige that brings with it sexual opportunities, if not sexual privileges. (O'Connell, 2016: 152)

---

[11] As I note in the Conclusion, marriage of course has implications for the men in the unions. However, this is beyond the scope of this Element.

The link between military service, masculinity, and marriage is not merely used to entice recruits – in many cases, marriage becomes an important part of the way the military regulates soldiers' lives. Studies of military management of marriage underscore how the measures taken to regulate soldiers' sexual activity include the creation of systems of sexual slavery (Soh, 2008), tolerating and regulating prostitution (Lie, 1997; Brathwaite, 2017; Roblin, 2018), and dictating whom soldiers can marry and the services provided to those partners (Branstetter, 1983; Zimmerman, 2020). Thus, the regulation of soldiers' sexual and romantic lives is often a way to bolster the ranks of the organization, as well as to maintain order within the group and cultivate loyalty to it. The prospect of maintaining military order by way of regulations on marriage relies on the idea that there are 'acceptable' and 'unacceptable' forms of marriage and masculinity – and the notion that the organization offers a path to the former.

Reform regarding military marriage regulations often came about not only because of shifting social or political mores but also because of assessments by military and political leaders that the benefits outweigh the costs for the military as an organization (Parsons, 2017).[12] Reflecting on the British Army in the Victorian era, Trustram (1984) notes that

> discussions on the desirability of increasing the married establishment and improving married provisions centered around three themes: firstly, the possibility of using the offer of improved marriage facilities as an incentive to recruitment and re-enlistment; secondly, the improvement to health, morale and morality which could be derived from what were seen as the steadying influences of marriage upon the licentious soldiery; and, thirdly, the use to which wives could be put as a cheap, well-disciplined labour for the regiment. (p. 39)

Lest we historicize state efforts to regulate the sexual and marital lives of soldiers, it is worth underscoring that modern militaries extend considerable effort managing marriages among soldiers. For example, the US military has reportedly provided more than a quarter of a million marital and relationship counseling sessions in recent years, representing a significant expenditure of time and resources (Kime, 2020). While some military organizations embrace marriage, others see it as incompatible with the military lifestyle and rely on single recruits. The French Foreign Legion's website, as of June 2023, states that the "lifestyle" of legionnaires "corresponds to that of a **single person**" (emphasis in original).[13]

---

[12] For a discussion of marriage, sexuality, and colonial regulations generally, see Voss (2008).

[13] The Foreign Legion's website further notes that members

Furthermore, as a venue for peer socialization, marriage can contribute to or detract from a military member's commitment to service.[14] Zimmerman notes that "West African administrators lauded mesdames tirailleurs," West African women who actively contributed to the colonial conquest through their relationships with West African men within the colonial branch of the French military, "as essential to troop retention and stabilization on colonial campaigns" (Zimmerman, 2020: 64). In the modern US Army, Family Readiness Groups (FRGs) are a form of support to military families that depends upon the uncompensated time and emotional labor of army spouses (generally the wives of servicemen). Gassman (2010) underscores that "Family members influence soldiers' decisions to enter and stay in the Army, and Family Readiness Groups became increasingly standardized as the Army sought, also increasingly, to protect its investment in soldiers willing and able to continue to serve" (p. 249). While designed to support military families, involvement in FRGs is also a way of socializing army spouses and of making service a family affair, with the objective of retaining soldiers. Failing to effectively engage military spouses can be detrimental to retention, as demonstrated by a study of the partners of British reservists and their spouses who were frustrated with "picking up the slack" at home during their partners' service (Basham and Catignani, 2018: 155). Thus, both formal marriage regulations and informal socialization processes shape the lives of military spouses, and especially military wives.

In short, we have compelling evidence that marriage has been and continues to be an important aspect of soldiers' lives that is subject to regulation by military higher-ups. These accounts suggest a cost-benefit analysis undergirding militaries' approach to marriage – an approach we will apply to rebel groups in the section on the STORM framework.

Military Wife, Military Life

Militaries' efforts to manage marriage have profound implications for the nonmilitary spouse in these unions (who is often, though certainly not universally, female), both in times of war and in times of peace. Feminist security scholars have identified how the concept of a "military wife" has been a way of

---

will only be allowed to marry after being in good standing with the following conditions:
– To serve under his true identity (thus to be regularized of military situation);
– having informed the command;
If he has less than 5 years of service he must obtain the authorization of the Minister of the Armed Forces. (Ministere des Armées, n.d.)

[14] For an interesting discussion of the ways in which both families and the military are 'greedy institutions', see Segal (1986).

militarizing women's lives, harnessing their (often unpaid) labor, and sustaining the war effort (Enloe, 2000). This organizational benefit is conditioned on women performing certain tasks and adopting certain behaviors. The socialization of women into their roles as "military wives" entails dressing and comporting themselves in a certain way; failure to conform can result in ostracization and can even imply ramifications for their partner's career. Within American military communities, derogatory terms (such as "dependapotamus")[15] and stereotypes (such as being unfaithful to deployed spouses) have emerged to police spouses' behavior (Cornelius and Monk-Turner, 2019).

The marriages and sexual relationships that soldiers have during war have implications for the postwar social, political, cultural, and legal order – and for women's lives especially. Consider, for example, the War Brides Act adopted by the United States in 1945, which paved the way for the immigration of more than 100,000 spouses and children associated with US servicemen abroad (Reimers, 1992: 22). Images of these foreign "war brides" became important political and cultural symbols; Simpson (2002) notes that "settling into domestic life in the 1950s, with little fanfare, as unfamiliar national subjects who had formerly been citizens of an enemy nation, Japanese war brides soon became meaningful figures in the discourse on racial integration and cultural pluralism" (p. 151), contributing to the debates about racial integration in the United States.

Zimmerman notes that there was greater support from the French colonial system to repatriate children that resulted from relationships between West African soldiers and Vietnamese women than to facilitate the movement of Vietnamese women to West Africa. Separating mothers from their children was a traumatic affair; she writes "the Vietnamese mothers who reported to ports to surrender their Afro-Vietnamese children to representatives of the French military did so in hysterics. Veteran Bakary Bieye believed that these women would have thrown themselves into the sea if there had not been a tall barrier at the quay" (Zimmerman, 2020: 191). Those family units that lived together in West Africa faced a series of challenges, including the difficulties of navigating significant cultural differences (Zimmerman, 2020).[16]

---

[15] Defined by OAF (Operation Allied Focus) Nation as "Dependapotamus: (noun) A shallow, heartless land mammal; preys upon enlisted military males; its natural habitat: the bars and nightclubs near military bases; its diet: government benefits, vodka and Doritos; its preferred transportation is a convertible adorned with military support stickers; its predominant predatory tactic is pre-emptive pregnancy and possessing your 1stSgt's digits on speed dial"; cited in Cornelius and Monk-Turner (2019: 241).

[16] Zimmerman (2020) notes that "the Vietnamese wives of African soldiers maintained relationships with the French state that survived the decolonization of Vietnam and the political independence of West African countries" (p. 193), observing that the French government continued to pay pensions to these women in the twenty-first century.

In summary, the literature on marriages and state militaries underscores the variation between countries and over time. It also highlights the ways in which marriage is a subject with implications for both organizational operations and individual experiences (particularly for women), both during and after war. With these dynamics in mind, we can now turn to the literature on rebel marriage specifically.

Rebel Marriage Systems at the Organizational Level

Though generally overlooked in the security studies literature, accounts examining rebel marriage have attributed these practices to a variety of rebel characteristics, including ideology, their efforts to recruit, retain, and control their members, and their system of governance in their areas of operations. In this section, I consider these explanations for rebel marriage regulations in turn and underscore the gaps in our current understanding.

A number of accounts underscore the relationship between rebels' approach to marriage and their ideology or organizational objectives. Donnelly (2018), for example, underscores the connection between gender norms and rebels' strategy and asserts that "if we do not see decisions about marriage as strategic, we miss key insights into a group's values and operations" (p. 460). Moghadam's (1995) study of revolutionary movements contrasts the "Women's Emancipation Model" of revolution with the "Woman-in-the-Family Model"; in the former, women are regarded "as part of the productive forces and citizenry, to be mobilized for economic and political purposes; she is to be liberated from patriarchal controls expressly for that purpose," whereas the latter "constructs an ideological linkage between patriarchal values, nationalism, and the religious order" and "assigns women the role of wife and mother, and associates women not only with family but with tradition, culture, and religion" (pp. 335–336). Rebel marriage policies may be an important articulation of rebels' gender ideology, defined as the "attitudes regarding the appropriate roles, rights, and responsibilities of women and men in society," and can thus play an important role in rebel governance or state-building (Kroska, 2007; Ahram, 2018).[17] Thus, the organizational objectives and beliefs of rebel groups shape their approach to marriage.

For example, reflecting on the policies of the LRA in Uganda, Baines (2014) notes that "the regulation of sexual relations became an organizing principle of the 'new Acholi' and forced marriage became a way of reproducing – literally giving birth to – the nation" (p. 406). Donnelly (2018) connects their system of

---

[17] Also H. Matfess, Sweet Nothings: Gender Ideology, Marriage, and Non-State Armed Groups' Recruitment Tactics (unpublished at the time of writing).

forced marriage and bans on extramarital sexual activity to their political objectives, underscoring how "the control of women's bodies and sexual behaviour was in line with the LRA's political goals because they wanted to protect the moral purity of the new Acholi nation they were trying to create" (p. 469). The system of courtship and marriage established by the rebels differed significantly from traditional Acholi culture; Baines (2014) notes that "the LRA both duplicates and purposefully violates Acholi sociality" (p. 409) through this practice in order to create this new society. As such, life in the rebellion was meaningfully structured around the family unit, with a system of forced marriage at its core.

Other rebel organizations' political objectives and ideological commitments lead them to never allow marriage or to approach the institution with skepticism. For example, though the organization has operated for decades, the Revolutionary Armed Forces of Colombia (FARC) has not permitted marriage among rebels. Rather than allowing marriages, the FARC established a system in which many "relationships were fixed term contracts" that could be dissolved by members of the relationship or by their military superiors (Gutiérrez-Sanín, 2018: 639).[18] Estrada-Fuentes (2016) relays an illustrative account from a female ex-combatant from the FARC who recalled:

> I had been in the guerrilla for about five years. I fell in love with a comrade I had been with for two years. But a snake bit me, and he was very anxious and worried and the commander didn't like it when a man cared like that for a woman, or the other way around, because they think that they will lose that combatant, that you are going to get bored in the guerrillas, lose morale, and that you will desert. So they sent him off and away from me. I was very sick. . . . He died in combat. I was very hurt. The commanders wouldn't tell me he was dead because they knew I was willing to die for him, and he felt the same. So they lied for a week. . . . I was depressed for seven months, but I could not let them know how I felt. The first day it was ok to show my sadness, but then I had to hide my feelings. They could get the wrong idea, that I wanted to desert, and they could kill me because of this. (p. 4)

Thus, romantic and sexual partnerships were permitted in the FARC but were carefully managed to discourage romance displacing commitment to the cause. Maintaining women's presence in the rebel group is an important component of the rebels' political project (as a leftist organization with a commitment to gender equality) but one that is threatened by romantic ties undermining

---

[18] Reports suggest a hierarchy of relationships in the FARC, ranging from short-term flings to more stable commitments, with varying degrees of interference from the FARC leadership, but underscore that "getting married was not an option in the FARC" (Mendez, 2012: 179). See also Kunz and Sjoberg (2009).

individual commitment to rebellion and the possibility of pregnancy reducing their readiness and fighting forces. To reduce the potential cost to the organization, the rebels strictly controlled the sexual activities of its members. Thus, even in a situation in which marriage was not permitted, the rebels' management of affairs of the heart should not be read to imply a laissez-faire approach to rebels' sex lives; rather, the FARC's admission of women and its regulations with respect to rebel sexuality reflect its efforts "to absorb the totality of the life of its fighters," fulfilling the rebels' ideological program (Sanín and Carranza Franco, 2017: 770–771). The FARC's approach to marriage reflects competing organizational interests and beliefs.

While rebels' belief systems and objectives exercise some influence over their approach to marriage, there is striking intra-ideological variation among groups. While the FARC's leftist ideology has been paired with a long-standing ban on marriage, other leftist groups like the CPN-M and the TPLF have allowed marriage.[19] One of the few comparative studies of rebel marriage, Donnelly's path-breaking study of the LRA and al-Shabaab argues that the system of forced marriage that rebel groups construct reflects whether they have an "ideology of social control" (meaning those who "are seeking to create an ideal community" and which Donnelly connects to religious and patriarchal beliefs) (Donnelly, 2019: 18) *and* the type of cohesion that they want to build, whether within the rebel group or by developing closer ties to the community (Donnelly, 2019: 17). Donnelly's work suggests that we must consider not only the beliefs of the rebels but also the operational considerations and personnel requirements of rebels if we are to understand their approach to marriage.

Indeed, a number of accounts suggest that rebels' marriage policies can attract recruits to the organization and encourage them to remain loyal to the rebellion (Marks, 2013; Hudson and Matfess, 2017). As I detail elsewhere, there are several ways that rebel groups can leverage grievances with marriage practices to facilitate recruitment: by providing resources to make it easier to get married, lowering the cost of marriage, identifying potential wives and arranging marriages, or offering a more appealing vision of marriage. Furthermore, these recruitment tactics can be used to attract support from both men and women.[20]

Of course, rebel groups are not only concerned with the *number* of recruits in their ranks; they are also concerned about the quality of these recruits and their commitment to the organization. Weinstein's foundational account of rebel recruitment suggests that material resources and incentives attract opportunistic – and thus perhaps low-quality – recruits (Weinstein, 2006). So, when rebel

---

[19] These groups will be discussed in greater detail in Section 3.
[20] In H. Matfess, Sweet Nothings: Gender Ideology, Marriage, and Non-State Armed Groups' Recruitment Tactics (unpublished at the time of writing).

groups provide tangible incentives to recruits, they must be wary of attracting flighty members. In order to account for the possibility of their marriage-related recruitment strategies attracting opportunistic members, it appears that rebel groups have adopted practices associated with marriage to render it both a recruitment tool and a screening mechanism. Forney (2015) notes that screening and "rites of passage" (p. 827) can impose costs on members that deter opportunistic recruits from committing to the organization. One of the ways that rebels can structure marriage recruitment policies to ensure that they are recruiting committed rebels is to put preconditions on marriage or to use it as a reward for service to the rebellion.[21] In the LRA, for example, the rebels' lack of "material wealth or popular support" resulted in the rebels using the allocation of wives as a reward system and incentive structure (Kramer, 2012: 28). Kramer (2012) notes

> To a large extent, women were allotted to males as a form of compensation and reward. As one of several tools of control, material rewards were promised to troops by LRA commanders upon military success ... the allocation of wives to male soldiers acted as a surrogate payment system in the absence of distributable material goods. Forced marriage functioned not only as a low-cost system of remuneration but also as a means of rewarding bravery and highlighting high status. (pp. 28–29)

In other instances, rebels have required that members serve for a certain number of years prior to being wed; in the LTTE, for example, one of the two partners had to have spent at least five years as a member (Thamizhini, 2020). These reforms reflect concerns about the effect of the institution of marriage on the durability of rebellion and the quality of the recruits.

As several accounts of rebel marriage systems underscore, marriage is not only a way of attracting members; it can also serve as a way in which the rebels maintain order and control within their ranks (Baines, 2014; Donnelly, 2019). Not only did the LRA's policies regarding marriage help reproduce the "New Acholi," but it also was designed to strengthen intra-rebel cohesion. The LRA's system of forced marriages "created dependence and loyalty to commanders in the LRA that transcended kinship lineages" (Baines, 2014: 411); furthermore "restricting sex outside of forced marriages may have been strategically beneficial for the LRA because it enforced the cohesion created through its marriage system" (Donnelly, 2018: 469). Marriage became a marker of intra-rebel hierarchy, as the number and individual characteristics of a man's wives reflected his status within the organization (Carlson and Mazurana, 2008).

---

[21] Though they must be careful to ensure that their preconditions are not more onerous than prevalent requirements for marriage.

Similarly, in Sierra Leone the Revolutionary United Front's approach to marriage contributed to the rise of a "parallel society in the bush" (Marks, 2013: 364). Marks (2013) notes that marriage served several objectives for the organization, particularly related to maintaining control and hierarchy within the organization:

> The RUF [Revolutionary United Front] top command framed marriage both as a right, in the entitlement expressed by commanders, and as a privilege for fighters. Men who could not provide food, clothes, shelter and security for their wife or girlfriend at the base or in secured towns were not supposed to keep wives. Young boy fighters also could not marry … In addition to signifying status and power within the group, marriage policies sought to impose order over combatants' personal lives, keeping camps tightly controlled amid the social upheaval of war. Highly bureaucratised channels were established to manage all aspects of life in the rebel group. (p. 367)

Yet, just as not all rebels see marriage or affection as furthering their political or ideological objectives, not all rebel groups see marriage as imparting greater control over their members. In some instances, romantic love and the desire to be married have been interpreted as threats to the cohesion and continuation of the rebellion. A defector named Makai from the National Liberation Front of Tripura (NLFT), a militant group in India, told the BBC in 2002, after surrendering to police, "I was fed up with killing people. I was fed up with running around in the jungles. When I fell in love with Sharmila [a female rebel], I was determined to marry her and flee." Makai and Sharmila were not the only members of the NLFT who fell in love and left the organization; the report notes that "after marriage, many of the guerrilla couples started fleeing from the bases and some of them surrendered" (Bhaumik, 2002). Those who were caught by the rebels were executed; not only did rebel leadership deem it necessary to kill those rebels but it also stopped accepting women into its ranks (Bhaumik, 2002). Thus, rebels falling in love, getting married, and seeking to leave the group was recognized as a significant threat to the rebels' activities and prompted a shift in their policies and practices. These changes had personnel and operational implications, particularly with respect to the inclusion of women and girls.

Weaving together the ways in which political objectives and operational concerns influence rebels' approach to marriage, recent studies connect rebels' marriage policies to their state-building (Ahram, 2018) and governance efforts. These are, of course, connected to groups' beliefs and political objectives but also reflect the organization's capability, material resources, and organizational capacity. As Giri (2023) notes, marriage and sexuality are not a mere side effect of governance but a key location where subjectivities are formed and controlled, which are vital to the political objectives of the rebel group. Moreover, intimate, sexual, and family life are intricately enmeshed in political projects such as nationhood, ethnicity, and religion require their collective reproduction in biological, legal, and cultural terms work through sex, gender, and marriage. (pp. 4–5)

Similarly, Ahram (2018) underscores that "rebel state-building is a distinctly gendered practice," meaning that the rebels' regulations regarding things like marriage are integral to such projects.

Rebel governance efforts can extend beyond the group's ranks to affect civilians' marriage practices and eligibility. Such governance can bolster or threaten the rebels' odds of survival and success. As Donnelly (2019) notes, the reception of community members to the rebels' marriage policies can have significant implications for the rebels' reputation and ability to operate. While some rebels' practices of marriage have led to community condemnation, other rebels have brokered important alliances through marriage. Consider, for example, the marriages of Mokhtar Belmokhtar ("a central player in the West African jihad") to Berber and Tuareg women, which "further extend his network in the Sahel".

Yet, as the literature on rebel governance and state-building in general underscores, aspirations and objectives alone cannot "deliver the goods," so to speak. Armed groups' capabilities, such as their degree of territorial control, extent and sources of funding, efforts to broker ties to the international community, and organizational infrastructure, shape the extent to which they can provide services and the manner in which they do so (see Mampilly, 2017; Florea, 2020; Huang and Sullivan, 2020; Loyle et al., 2021). With this in mind, we must also consider how the rebels' material conditions and operational concerns shape the nature of their regulation of marriage.

Worth noting is that once a decision with respect to managing marriage is made by rebel leaders, it is not an ossified feature of rebel life – rebels can shift their approach to marriage over time. Leaders in the Hukbalahap Rebellion (also called the Huks) in the Philippines, for example, were initially skeptical of marriage before eventually adopting policies to permit and regulate unions. Huk leadership first understood rebels' sexual appetites and romantic attachments as a threat to the rebellion's cohesion and reputation among civilians (Gayer, 2013: 353).[22] Pomeroy, an American veteran who became an important leader in the

---

[22] Lanzona (2009) notes that extramarital affairs among the rebels were used as evidence that Huks were "sexual predators" and to discredit the entire movement (p. 124). Similarly, Goodwin (1997) notes that the "sex problem" was a source of internal strife and criticism from "families in the barrios" (p. 60).

movement, wrote that the leadership recognized that "relationships spring up [within the movement], they cannot be denied. So if they are going to exist they must be controlled" (Pomeroy, 2011: 142). In this case, we see a change adopted in response to a recognition of the limits of the rebels' control.

Furthermore, there can be a wide chasm between rebel leaders' platonic ideal of marriage and the realities of these unions. To adopt Wood's parlance, the "policies" and "practices" of marriage may differ (Wood, 2018). Reflecting on the practice of 'revolutionary marriage' among the leftist Naxalbari uprising, Roy (2006) observes that "movement participants defied the institution of marriage as they did with all other social institutions, displaying their revolutionary zeal and progressive nature . . . The rejection of traditional arranged marriages to emphasize partnerships based on love, equality and comradeship is accompanied by a rejection of both the religious and civil nature of marriage" (p. 103). Yet Roy (2006) underscores that these marriages often fell short of the rebels' lofty ideals. She writes:

> Women's narratives often voice betrayal, disappointment and anger at the way in which everyday life remained unchanged even though they "married" so-called political men . . . The contradiction between men's public and private lives comes out forcefully in their accounts on conjugality. While male activists were urged to renounce the role of the "householder" for that of the "revolutionary", women were expected to conform to middle-class norms and expectations of domesticity and womanhood. (p. 109)

As such, our investigation of marriage in rebel groups must go beyond the formal policies articulated by rebels to consider the ways in which marriage is experienced by those the union binds together (see Wood, 2018).

Individual Implications: The Postwar Significance of Rebel Marriages

Wartime unions have long-lasting legacies; attitudes, institutions, traumas, and social ties associated with rebel marriages often persist into the post-conflict period (Huang, 2017: Zaks, 2017; Lazarev, 2019; Themnér and Karlén, 2020). These legacies can manifest in forced and voluntary marriages, as well as in those unions that continue into the postwar period and those that are terminated shortly after (or during) the war.

The ways in which marriages originate may not determine how they are eventually experienced by spouses. Consider Amina Ali, one of the Chibok Schoolgirls abducted by Boko Haram in Northern Nigeria in 2014, who eventually escaped with the man she had been forcibly married to within the group. She told CNN that they were separated and that "I'm not comfortable with the way I'm being kept from him" and addressed him directly, saying "I want you to know that I'm still thinking about you, and just because we are separated doesn't mean I have forgotten about you" (Busari and Jones, 2016). One study of marriage under the Khmer Rouge found that these unions were just as stable as other marriage cohorts in Cambodia – despite the fact that these marriages were coerced and out of line with Cambodian courtship practices (Heuveline and Poch, 2006).

The termination of wartime marriages can have profound implications for women's lives and well-being, divorcing them not only from their partner but also from wartime gender norms and relations. Consider postwar Eritrea, where marriages between male and female members of the Eritrean People's Liberation Front (EPLF) often ended in divorce.[23] In the early years of Eritrean independence, the *Washington Post* reported

> in a scathing editorial in the government-run newspaper earlier this year, Askalu Mankerios, head of the women's union, accused the Liberation Front's male fighters of succumbing to family pressures to conform to traditions, often at the expense of their female comrades. She cited cases in which men divorced the wives they had married in the field for younger women who cooked, wore their hair long and more often than not were the virgins that Eritrean society prefers as brides. (Parmelee, 1993)

Such divorces represented a sharp break from wartime patterns, where women were lauded for taking on traditional male tasks and defying gender norms. A female veteran of the EPLF lamented that the termination of wartime unions was another manifestation of female veterans' postwar marginalization:

> You have to start thinking about really unimportant things, like how to dress your daughter and yourself, since the neighbors are watching and we are not allowed to walk in combat uniform any more, we are not allowed to parade in our uniforms during the victory parade. We have [to] wear traditional dress and behave like traditional women. Do you know that more than 80 percent of marriages between fighters are now divorced. The men are all looking for traditional wives in the village, they don't want their female comrades any more. (Weber, 2011: 363)

Male former fighters confirmed these perceptions; male ex-combatants of the EPLF told one researcher that female fighters were not sufficiently feminine or modest to be wives (Mehreteab, 2002). The dissolution of wartime unions of EPLF fighters not only left individual women in economically precarious situations; it also reflected a shift in society's willingness to accept the gender-deviant behavior that women had engaged in as members of the rebellion.

---

[23] Quoted in Weber (2011: 361).

These changes hint at the stigma that women formerly associated with rebel groups may face in the postwar period.

Wartime marriages often exert considerable influence on the perception of former rebel women,[24] affecting their ability to reintegrate. The stigma that former rebel wives face as a result of their wartime activities and relationships can make it more difficult for them to find a new partner and participate in their community. For example, some women previously with the LRA struggle to find husbands, despite expressing an interest in doing so. These women's marriage prospects were hampered by community perceptions about their morality and character (see Institute for War and Peace Reporting, 2007). While mistrust and stigma did not necessarily *prevent* all former LRA wives from remarrying, there is some evidence that these women can end up settling for unions in which the traditional courtship and marriage rituals were not completed. One study found that many of these women remarried through elopement; it notes that

> only two participants, both still married to their LRA husbands, had their bridewealth completed. The eventual completion of bridewealth by the partner to the ex-abductee's family is the ultimate goal, and in this regard, we recorded the two women as having achieved formal marriages and the rest as having failed to secure culturally acceptable marriages at the time of the interviews. (Kiconco and Nthakomwa, 2018: 69)

This style of marriage has implications for the social status of both the husband and the wife, as well as for the legitimacy of the marriage in the eyes of the community. Kiconco and Nthakomwa (2018) note that

> women's families do not fully respect their husbands. In relation to marriage as a determinant of successful recovery and reintegration, as with their peers in elopements, women in cohabitation unions have also not obtained a formal position in their new societal context as married women and mothers. Until their bridewealth is fully paid, their position in their marital family and villages remains unsecured and uncertain. (p. 69)

---

[24] There has also been discrimination against male rebels. Suarez and Baines (2021) feature the experience of OM, a man formerly associated with the LRA, who told them that "none of the reception centres had a positive view about men who reproduced with these women. They were told that their husbands forced them into the relationship … They also look at most of us like perpetrators. [They would say] 'you cannot marry a killer, you need to get someone who is your age and able to take care of you'" (p. 15). This negative stereotype about men in the LRA overlooks how forced marriage can represent a form of violence against men, as well as the roles that some husbands played in arranging or encouraging an exit from the armed group for their wives and children, and the peer networks that rebel marriages constituted. In OM's case, Suarez and Baines (2021) note that because he was barred from seeing his children, "he arranged secret meetings with the mother of his children to receive updates" (p. 16) on how they were.

Furthermore, accounts of women who left the LRA with their children born of wartime unions underscore the perilous social position they and their children navigate. While some women have sought to provide for themselves and their children absent any assistance or recognition from the father or paternal family, in other cases "the importance of paternal identity in Acholi" encourages women to connect with the child's father and family, so as to not contribute to "a child's sense of not belonging" (Oliveira and Baines, 2021: 763).

In other instances, some wartime marriages have proven durable and have bolstered women's prospects and status after war. Writing on Ketiba Banat, the women's wing of the Sudan People's Liberation Army (SPLA), Pinaud (2015) notes that:

> The signing of the 2005 CPA especially bolstered their ascension. Their husbands became members of the new Government of Southern Sudan. For example in 2009–2010, both the Minister of Information and the Minister of Cooperation were married to Ketiba Banat recruits, and so was the Chairperson of the Ministry of Widows. The former recruits benefited from the 25% positive discrimination, used by the elite to appoint their wives and the lower strata's, to army and government positions. They were often promoted to important positions in the Police, prisons or various ministries. In 2010, thirty-six of them worked in the Police, twenty-six for different Ministries, twenty-three in the Prisons, only ten in the SPLA, and four for the Ministry of Wildlife. (p. 386)

Thus, these women's wartime marriages provided them with post-conflict economic security and status.

Whether or not a female rebel is married, to whom she is married, and the nature of this marriage are all relevant dimensions for understanding women's wartime experiences and their post-conflict prospects. Though we have clear evidence regarding the difficulties and opportunities that female ex-combatants and rebel wives face after war, we lack a framework to help us trace how the features of wartime marriages among rebels affect these women during and after war.

Concluding Notes

Rebel groups adopt a wide variety of approaches to marriage and can change their approach over time. Efforts to understand this variation are still a relatively new area of study. The literature that has engaged with rebel marriage typically is focused on case studies,[25] rather than comparative analysis, and often examines instances of forced or coerced marriage (See Goodwin, 1997; Annan et al., 2009; Coulter, 2009; Baines, 2014; Pinaud, 2015; Hynd, 2016; Hudson and Matfess, 2017). Despite the limited comparative work done on the subject,

---

[25] With some cases receiving a disproportionate share of attention, such as the LRA.

synthesizing the case studies on marriage in rebel groups reveals some areas of consensus that provide a foundation for a broader study of this phenomenon. Furthermore, examining military management of marriage also provides us with a background for understanding the importance of marriage for organizations at war.

There is no clear-cut or singular explanation for how rebels approach and manage marriage. Any examination of this phenomenon must account for a variety of rebel concerns and characteristics. As Donnelly (2018) concludes, the LRA's forced marriage system "was a benefit to the group for many potential reasons, including serving as a reward system for men, to reinforce its political goals and to create cohesion" (p. 471). As the following section on the Strategies and Tactics of Rebel Marriage (STORM) describes, I suggest that understanding rebel marriage systems requires considering not only rebels' political objectives and belief systems but also the dynamics of internal cohesion and membership retention, as well as the rebels' logistical concerns. Rebels' regulations on marriage may vary over time, as the conditions in which the group is operating shift or the priorities of the organization change. The following section will introduce the Strategies and Tactics of Rebel Marriage (STORM) framework to facilitate an understanding variation in rebel groups' marriage practices at the organizational level.

The Strategies and Tactics of Rebel Marriage

> The people were not only fighting with the police or reactionary, feudal agents, but they were also breaking the feudal chains of exploitation and oppression and a whole cultural revolution was going on among the people. Questions of marriage, questions of love, questions of family, questions of relations between people. All of these things were being turned upside down and changed in the rural areas.
>
> (Pettigrew and Shneiderman, 2004: n.p.)

This section introduces the Strategies and Tactics of Rebel Marriage (STORM) framework. This framework facilitates an understanding of the variety of approaches that rebel groups have taken towards regulating marriage, changes in their policies over time, and the implications of these policies for women's participation in political violence.[26] The STORM framework rests on the assumption that rebel leaders weigh the potential costs and benefits of marriage across several dimensions when determining how to approach this issue organizationally.

The STORM framework draws from the literature's discussion of the role of ideology, cohesion, and reputational concerns as drivers of rebel decisions about

---

[26] I consider here only heterosexual marriages; future work can be done to consider how non-state armed groups approach same-sex and queer relationships.

marriage; case study accounts of rebels deliberating the feasibility and desirability of marriage within their ranks; as well as the discussion about the ways in which state-affiliated militaries shifted their approach to marriage in order to attract recruits, maintain morale among servicepeople, and support the operations of the military organization. This framework thus emerged from a synthesis of the literature on marriage in wartime, among both state and non-state armed groups. The STORM framework is inductive in that it reflects the limitations of the extant data (discussed in the Introduction to this Element and in subsequent subsections of this section); despite these limitations, I believe that this framework improves upon the state of the literature by providing us with the tools to examine drivers of variation both within and between groups over time.

This framework suggests that rebels' marriage practices reflect a process of weighing the costs and benefits of marriage as it relates to three broad concerns:

(1) the relationship between the gender norms practiced in prevalent marriage dynamics and the rebels' broader political project;
(2) the anticipated effect of marriage on cohesion within and loyalty to the organization; and
(3) whether marriage will be considered a boon to or a drain on rebels' resources and logistical capabilities.

Following the introduction of this framework and a discussion of the potential benefits and drawbacks of marriage for each of these concerns, I unpack its utility for our understanding of rebel organizational considerations and for women's experiences as rebels through a brief comparison of the marriage policies of five rebel groups.

While this section often presents marriage as a bureaucratic matter of rebel strategy and focuses primarily on the organizational unit of analysis, we should not overlook how these unions can be the site of profound human connection, affection, and even love. Consider Pomeroy's assertion – while navigating the forests of the Philippines as a member of the Hukbalahap Rebellion, coping with the harsh environment, surviving off of limited rations, helping organize a rebellion, and dodging attack from the government forces – that "there is no greater horror than these episodes in which Celia's [his wife and a fellow leader in the rebellion] life is threatened and I am impotent to go to her aid" (Pomeroy, 2011: 206). These unions – and the emotions that may develop within them – have operational significance for the rebels and often have personal significance for individual members. The following section will draw out more clearly the individual-level implications of wartime rebel marriage practices for female ex-rebels after war, expanding on the brief discussion on individual-level dynamics discussed in this section.

Introducing the Strategies and Tactics of Rebel Marriage (STORM) Framework

I consider three general, possible benefits of marriage for rebel groups: that it will help the rebels further their political project, that it will promote loyalty to the organization and facilitate recruitment of new members, and that it will improve the rebels' logistical capabilities and reputation among the civilian population. I also consider three ways by which marriage may undermine rebels' objectives along these three dimensions: that it will replicate or entrench gender relations or social norms that the rebels seek to overturn or that are in contravention of their ideology, that it will displace rebels' commitment to the cause with commitment to a partner, and that the logistical burden of managing the reproductive lives of married rebels will detract from their military efforts or degrade their reputation among civilians.

Reassessments of the relative costs and benefits of marriage in each of these three categories can occur throughout the course of the conflict, producing changes in how rebel groups approach marriage over time. Where marriage once constituted an insurmountable logistical burden, an intolerable drain on military resources, or an impediment to the actualization of the rebels' political project, it may eventually become a regulated and endorsed feature of rebel life. As such, the rebel groups discussed in the following subsections do not fit neatly into "ideal types" that correspond to the individual cells in Table 1. Rather, we can see how changes in the assessment of the threats and opportunities that marriage presents across these three dimensions change how rebels approach marriage. These categories are overlapping and interdependent: rebels' broader political project can condition the anticipated effect on rebel cohesion and the anticipated logistical implications can override ideological or cohesion-related concerns. The framework developed in this section is intended to be an analytical tool for understanding how rebels approach marriage, rather than serving as a formula for predicting a static set of policies or attitudes. In what follows, I briefly introduce the considerations in each of the columns described in Table 1.

Relationship to the Broader Political Project

Marriage is a profoundly political phenomenon that can reflect or challenge broader gendered power dynamics. Rebels' management of marriage gives them an opportunity to actualize a part of their broader political project by implementing a form of marriage that corresponds with their preferred gender roles for men and women (Donnelly, 2019: 17). Whether rebels are concerned with enforcing traditional gender roles, cultivating separate spheres for men and women, articulating a new form of womanhood, or promoting women's

Table 1 The Strategies and Tactics of Rebel Marriage (STORM) framework

	The Relationship to the Broader Political Project	The Effect on Internal Cohesion	The Logistics of Marriage
Costs	Prevalent marriage practices and associated gender roles are incompatible with rebels' political project.	Commitment to partner/family overrides commitment to cause; marriage and affection encourage defection.	Rebels lack organizational, logistical, or material resources to successfully regulate marriage. Marriage may deplete manpower of rebel group. Marriage can undermine relationships with the civilian population.
Benefits	Rebels' political project is compatible with gender norms associated with prevalent marriage practices.	Marriage promotes loyalty to organizations (improving retention) or attracts new recruits (this can require a reinterpretation of practices).	Marriage promotes better relations with surrounding communities, making it easier to operate. Marriage incorporates women into logistical duties and social reproduction within organization.

equality with men, their approach to marriage provides an opportunity to foster these norms and enforce certain standards of behavior. In some instances, marriage becomes central to rebel life as a part of actualizing their political agenda, whereas in other circumstances rebels are skeptical of marriage or bar it entirely. Marriage practices may be reinterpreted by the rebels in order to align with their political project.[27] By acting as a way in which rebels can prescribe their preferred gender roles, marriage can further the rebels' political project (Ahram, 2018; Donnelly, 2019).

Cohesion within Rebellion and Retention

Participation in a rebel group is a high-risk endeavor with little prospect for direct reward (Wood, 2003); rebellions depend, to some degree, on cultivating commitment to a cause greater than oneself. In so doing, rebel leaders must be mindful of competing loyalties and attendant to new ways of fostering commitment to the cause. Romantic partners can represent a potent threat to rebel commitment or these unions can be leveraged to produce an even greater commitment to the rebellion by tying their marriage to the organization. The specific ways in which marriage is practiced within the rebel group may reflect efforts to reduce the possibility that marriage will detract from commitment to the rebellion; reinterpretations of marriage practices in the group can tie the possibility of marriage to group membership to promote cohesion within the rebellion and retention of rebels. Similarly, marriage may be designed in a manner that reduces the possibility of defection.

Logistical Implications

Rebel groups' approach to marriage is also dependent on the calculations of how different marriage policies will fit in with the rebels' logistical needs and capabilities. Marriage can be a means by which rebel groups augment their logistical capabilities, as the incorporation of women via marriage can improve relations with civilians and can allow the rebels to delegate tasks to wives. Rebel groups may need to have a degree of organizational capacity and a sufficient resource base to allow and regulate marriages. The very management of rebel marriage scan require resources and organizational capacity that rebels may struggle to muster during war. Furthermore, as we have seen, marriage can decrease manpower by encouraging defection, degrading the organization's operational capacity. For most rebel groups, marriage will come with both

---

[27] Some have described this as the "gender ideology" of the organization (see Asal, Avdan, and Shuaibi, 2020; Matfess, n.d.)

logistical costs and benefits and will require rebels to balance these conditions, along with the anticipated effects of marriage on cohesion and the rebels' political project.

Case Studies

In the remainder of the section, I use illustrative examples from the Tigray People's Liberation Front (TPLF), the Liberation Tigers of Tamil Eelam (LTTE), the Maoists in Nepal (CPN-M), al-Shabaab and the Islamic State to demonstrate the utility of this framework.

This selection of cases allows me to consider variation between and within ideologies, regions, and time periods. For example, though the TPLF, CPN-M, FARC, and the Huks are all leftist groups, they all took different approaches to marriage. Similarly, al-Shabaab and the Islamic State both fall within the same broad ideological category of religious extremist rebel groups (and, more specifically, Salafi-jihadist rebels) but have not adopted identical practices for marriage. The LTTE and the TPLF were both influenced by nationalist objectives but adopted different policies with respect to marriage. Both changes within groups over time and this intra-ideological variation highlight that, while ideology can certainly shape groups' marriage policies and practices, it is not a reliable predictive tool. In this framework, I suggest that we look instead to the "political project" of the rebels, which includes context-specific objectives that may not be considered in traditional constructions of "ideology" (such as gender ideology or culturally relevant appeals) and which can allow for intra-ideological variation. As illustrated in Table 2, the nonreligious rebel groups have fairly high proportions (Loken and Matfess, 2023) of women in their ranks as combatants, noncombatants, and leaders, whereas the religious groups include women less frequently in combat and leadership roles. These cases also provide me with the opportunity to understand the conditions under which certain rebel groups have shifted their approach to marriage over time. The higher-than-average prevalence of women in these organizations reflects my focus on marriages *within the group*.[28]

Furthermore, the cases discussed here also reflect the availability of information about these groups' marriage practices. To collect data for this project, I draw from fieldwork in Ethiopia,[29] firsthand accounts published in English, and secondary literature. Given these data limitations, it is important to note that this section is aimed at probing an understudied phenomenon and providing

---

[28] Of course, determining what constitutes membership versus association is a tricky endeavor and beyond the scope of this Element. For work on the dynamics of membership, see Loken (2022).

[29] Interviewees from this fieldwork are identified as "Respondent" with a randomly generated number. These interviews were approved by the Yale University IRB #2000026832.

Table 2 Summary of case-study rebel groups

Group Name	Primary Areas of Operations	Ideology (as Listed in FORGE)	Founding Year (as Listed in FORGE)	Female Combatants as Listed in WAAR (Prevalence)	Female Noncombatants as Listed in WAAR (Prevalence)	Female Leaders as Listed in WAAR and (Prevalence)
TPLF	Ethiopia	Communist and Nationalist	1975	Yes (High)	Yes (High)	Yes (Moderate)
CPN-M	Nepal	Communist	1995	Yes (High)	Yes (High)	Yes (High)
LTTE	Sri Lanka	Nationalist	1976	Yes (High)	Yes (High)	Yes (Moderate)
al-Shabaab	Somalia	Religious	2008	Yes (Occasional)	Yes (High)	Yes (Occasional)
Islamic State	Iraq	Religious	2000	Yes (Occasional)	Yes (Moderate)	Yes (Occasional)

Note: Please see Loken and Matfess (2023) – the Women's Activities in Armed Rebellion (WAAR) codebook – for details on prevalence coding.

a framework for grappling with variation – it is not an attempt to unpack causal mechanisms or make definitive claims about rebel groups' approaches to marriage. As Giri (2023) notes, there is a critical need for future research to identify the scope conditions under which rebel organizations are likely to adopt marriage policies.

Admitting that my case selection strategy is a function of the availability of information makes me want to instinctively duck and cover to avoid being pelted with insults by Very Serious Academics™.[30] While certainly suboptimal from a methodological perspective, such an approach is often a necessity for those working on subjects that have been relegated to the margins for being too feminine or unserious for traditional security studies.[31] Despite these limitations, at the very least I hope that this will serve as a brush-clearing exercise so that others may contribute to this nascent field of studies. Marriage and war are both deeply human and messy phenomena; the selection of case studies.

The Tigray People's Liberation Front (TPLF)

In the early years of the TPLF's activities, marriage was banned for members. There were a variety of justifications for this ban. One such justification was that marriage could "distract" from their objective "to destroy and overthrow the Derg" (Veale, 2003: 32). Additionally, the subordination of wife to husband that often accompanies traditional heterosexual marriage arrangements was incompatible with the gender-egalitarian ideology espoused by the TPLF. Not only was the rebels' skepticism about marriage in the first years of the war connected to their political project but it was a way of attracting support and recruits by helping some women avoid unwanted marriages. One former fighter recalled, "I had an older and younger brother. They were allowed to go to school, but I was not because I was a girl. My parents were planning to marry me to someone when I was 13, so I ran away and joined the TPLF. Because of the TPLF, I have my freedom" (Negewo–Oda and White, 2011: 173).[32] In recruiting women on this basis, the rebels bonded their freedom to their identity as a rebel, as well as making good on their claims of supporting gender egalitarianism.

Importantly, the TPLF expended energy regulating rebels' romantic lives even when marriage was not permitted. Female veterans of the TPLF recounted

---

[30] If not insults perhaps copies of Designing Social Inquiry (King, Keohane, and Verba, 2021).

[31] In some instances, participants in these marriages themselves have discouraged the study of rebel marriage; Gayer (2012) suggests "a universal tendency, among women militants, to disentangle their affective and political careers in their testimonies, in order to distance themselves from traditional perceptions of women as emotive beings" (p. 119).

[32] See also Hammond (1990).

that prior to the lifting of the ban on marriage they were given "lessons on how to control pregnancy, both using contraception pills and natural methods" (Veale, 2003: 64) and that women who became pregnant had abortions.[33] Given the rebels' resources at the time, it appears that providing instruction and contraceptives was a more viable approach than attempting to care for children and new mothers.

However, the TPLF changed course in the mid-1980s with respect to its policies on marriage. Just as there were a number of reasons for banning marriage, there were a variety of justifications for allowing it. The TPLF's shift corresponded to changes in the balance of power between the rebels and the government; at the time that the rebels changed their policies with regard to marriage and childbirth, they had significant territorial control and could develop an infrastructure to manage rebel marriage and ensure the safety of young children and pregnant women.[34] Furthermore, the TPLF's "hotly debated" decision to lift its ban on marriage in part reflected that "the pressure to legalize marriage was mounting as most of TPLF fighters were youngsters in their early twenties" and "the pressure coming from the increase of young unmarried girls as a result of the flow of the male youngsters to the ranks of the TPLF" (Berhe, 2018: 137–138). Thus, the reform to allow marriage reflected concerns about internal cohesion. As one veteran noted, there were demands from community members that the TPLF "replace" the youths who had been killed in the war against the Derg.[35] Changing marriage policy was apparently important for the TPLF to maintain good relations with civilians, a critical part of the rebels' military strategy and a condition for their continued operations. Additionally, the marriage policy reflected (or was justified by) a shift in the rebels' gender ideology. One high-ranking woman in the TPLF told a foreign journalist that the rebels' approach to "the woman question" had been "emphasising the combat side too much" (Hammond, 1989: 69) and that allowing marriage was a part of rectifying that imbalance. She further noted that this policy involved shifting women's contributions away from combat roles and towards positions managing the areas under the rebels' control (Hammond, 1989: 69).

The TPLF's version of marriage was qualitatively different from the types of marriages practiced in prewar Tigray – both among rebels and in rebel-held territory, the rebels implemented minimum ages of marriage for girls and the marriages were purported to be more egalitarian than civilian unions (Veale, 2005). The TPLF's "democratic marriages" could be seen as a reinterpretation of marriage to ensure that rebels' marriages were bound up in their commitment

---

[33] Respondent 68 in author fieldwork.   [34] Respondent 7 in author fieldwork.
[35] Respondent 37 in author fieldwork.

to the rebels' struggle and to ensure that the practice of marriage was in line with the rebels' political project. Such reinterpretations seek to tie rebels' intimate relationships to their commitment to the rebellion, rendering them as complementary rather than substitute goods. Of course, these relationships were also the site of profound affection and comfort for some of the couples, such as Mariam and Fikru, who dreamed of what their life together would be like after war.

Not all of the members of the TPLF were thrilled about these changes. Many female fighters in the TPLF protested the decision to repeal the ban on marriage, fearing that marriage and pregnancy would pull them away from their prestigious work as combatants and force them into less prestigious staff positions and motherhood.[36] As one female veteran recalled, many of the women believed "we will be mothers, be pregnant – not be a fighter."[37] Some of the fighters resisted the change in order to remain dedicated to the fight; one female veteran recalled some taking the position that "I have buried my friends and I will not marry until the enemy is dismissed [defeated]."[38] This attitude suggests that some women believed that being a wife would undermine their ability to be a fighter and detract from their ability to contribute to the struggle. A high-ranking male veteran recalled that there was a qualitative shift in attitudes following the change, not only changes in personnel policies. He recalled that "we male fighters started being like our fathers and the women were like their mothers," though "before that we were comrades on equal footing."[39] Marriage, for some TPLF fighters, was incongruent with the rebels' commitment to gender egalitarianism.

Though the reform was, at least partially, informed by the rebels' need to maintain good relations with the peasantry in order to operate effectively, new logistical challenges emerged after the change. These challenges included socializing rebels into what a proper "democratic marriage" entailed (Teklu, 2015). One female veteran recalled that the TPLF released some guidance to its fighters about proper courtship, including the suggestion that partners date for six months before marriage, and how to celebrate their nuptials.[40] Another female veteran recalled that a marriage for fighters meant maybe getting a new dress uniform or a slight increase in rations and noted that wedding nights were often spent in plastic tents because fighters did not have property.[41] Democratic marriages, it would appear, were modest ones but still demanded a degree of management by rebel leadership.

---

[36] Respondent 8 and Respondent 76 in author fieldwork.
[37] Respondent 76 in author fieldwork.   [38] Respondent 37 in author fieldwork.
[39] Respondent 31 in author fieldwork.   [40] Respondent 26 in author fieldwork.
[41] Respondent 27 in author fieldwork.

The Communist Party of Nepal – Maoists (CPN-M)

The CPN-M's regulation of marriage reflected its revolutionary aspirations and political project. Hisila Yami, a high-ranking member of the CPN-M (who married another prominent figure in the movement) noted in her autobiography that "in a society where polygamous relationships existed despite legal penalizations, and men could easily get away with infidelity, it was natural that the Maoist movement in Nepal would be faced with concerns regarding marriage, love, and sexual relationships" (Yami, 2021: 131). The rebels sought to eliminate gender and intercaste discrimination through many of their internal policies, including their regulations on marriage. The very language the rebels used to justify their model of marriage reflected the rebels' broader progressive, modernizing revolutionary project. In Nepal, "janabadi" marriages that crossed caste and ethnicity were a part of the revolutionary project (Sthapit and Doneys, 2017). Furthermore, reflecting the rebels' political objectives, they also raised the minimum age of marriage and substituted traditional Hindu marriage rituals for a long engagement, party approval, and a pledge of fidelity to the party and the cause (Gayer, 2013). For example, Gayer (2013) noted that the CPN-M took a "scientific" approach to the issue, concluding that the rebels were better off not trying to prevent something as "natural" as marriage, while recognizing that the expectations placed upon wives and mothers were a threat to women's participation in the rebellion (p. 348).

Though the rebels acknowledged love an important aspect of these unions, the party's habit of posting married couples apart from one another also suggests a concern with preventing familial duties from overshadowing commitment to the party (Gayer, 2013). Gayer notes that "love marriages" "came with certain caveats, the most significant of which being the pre-eminence of party concerns over romantic and family matters – a conscious attempt at preventing 'libidinal withdrawal' from the movement" (Gayer, 2013: 348). The practice of posting partners far from one another allowed the rebels to undermine the gendered division of labor that often accompanies marriage, which was out of step with the rebels' progressive ideology (Gayer, 2013). Gayer (2013) further notes that "The alleged objectives of the Maobadis' 'scientific' approach towards 'love–marriage–sex' were to contain sexual anarchy within the movement, while protecting women against unwanted pregnancies and premature retirement" (p. 350). To that end, he observes that the party encouraged safe sex among married couples to prevent pregnancy from curtailing women's political activities (Gayer, 2013).

The CPN-M also reinterpreted marriage practices to tie marriage to the rebellion and to retain rebels, particularly women, in the movement. Retaining women was of particular interest, given that women in the CPN-M were regarded (at least according to some reports) as even more committed to the rebellion than their male counterparts. Furthermore, the inclusion of women "had a positive impact on cohesion within the CPN-M and the allegiance of men" (Giri and Haer, 2021: 12). Giri and Haer (2021) cite a high-ranking leader who asserted "in many cases, because of women, men stayed in the group. Whole families were devoted to the party" (p. 12). Giri notes that the rebels also worked to ensure that the death of a partner only drew members closer to the rebellion; he notes that "the loss of a partner in combat was used by the Maoists as an opportunity to engender a sense of vengeance and anger in the widow/widower against the government forces".

The model of marriage practiced by the rebels may have also raised the cost of defection for women. Giri and Haer (2021) suggest that part of the reason for women's acute commitment to the rebellion was not only because of the gender-egalitarian aspirations of the rebels but also because the costs of leaving the rebels were especially high for female rebels who "security forces could readily identify . . . as Maoists, and they could face torture, rape, and potential death" (p. 11). Beyond these immediate physical threats, would-be defectors also faced the possibility of social stigma, which may be especially severe for female ex-combatants given their gender-bending activities and participation in intercaste marriages (Upreti and Shivakoti, 2018). Pettigrew and Shneiderman go so far as to suggest that the CPN-M's encouragement of marriage among young female members was a way of preventing female rebels from leaving and bringing these young women further under the control of the organization (Pettigrew and Shneiderman, 2004). Certainly, the threat to women's liberty that marriage presented did not stop CPN-M leadership from encouraging young female members to get married, reflecting a reality in which "unmarried women draw lots of suspicion from men as well as women for their unmarried status," threatening cohesion and the actualization of the rebels' objectives (Parvati, 2003). Still, many marriages among combatants were also motivated by profound affection for one another; Yami's autobiography speaks fondly of her husband, their courtship, and the ways in which their differing personalities but shared commitment to the cause made for an eventful life together (Yami, 2021).

Marriages among CPN-M members also helped the rebels build their base of support among civilians. Yami recalls that "there was such a close relationship between the Indian Nepali community and our party" that high-ranking members of the CPN-M "even got their daughters married to students in Siliguri" (Yami, 2021: 102). Furthermore, according to a female fighter, women's participation in the group (which was facilitated by the rebels' marriage policy), helped the rebels cultivate legitimacy among civilians; she told researchers, absent women, the rebels "would have been a roving guerrilla cut off from the people" (Giri and Haer, 2021: 13). Though the rebels' marriages came with clear logistical benefits, the practice of regularly separating spouses suggests that no small degree of organization and effort went into managing married couples.

The Liberation Tigers of Tamil Eelam (LTTE)

As in the TPLF, marriage was initially banned for members of the LTTE. "Many eyebrows were raised" when the ban on marriage within the LTTE was lifted in response to an elite LTTE member falling in love; indeed, following the change "there was bitterness among some of the senior cadres who had renounced their romance for rebellion," suggesting another way that removal of bans can sow discord within the ranks of non-state armed groups (Swamy, 2003: 114). Even after marriage was permitted within the groups ranks, it was reportedly a contentious subject – accounts differ about the extent to which rebels endorsed marriage and who in the organization was encouraged to wed. Balasingham's autobiography recalls that the "most senior women's commander" was often present at weddings she attended and that the woman's "broad smile always indicated her pleasure at seeing the young female fighters under her command, getting married" (Balasingham, 2001: 340). Another account recalls that debates over who could get married could threaten the cohesion within the leadership's ranks; Thamizhini (2020) writes that

> difficult predicaments often arose when many older male fighters requested permission to marry very young female fighters. However, the final deciding authority rested with the female commanders in the matter. It was also common that conflict arose when male colonels tried to apply pressure on behalf of their cadres. This created a lot of stress for the female commanders as well. (p. 81)

Rebel leadership seems to have maintained a somewhat skeptical approach to marriage among the rank-and-file, alluding to a different cost-benefit analysis for marriage among different ranks of members.[42] According to Gayer (2013), "not only did the LTTE try to discourage their fighters from getting married too early, they also gave them the opportunity – and possibly encouraged them – to leave their children in the hands of the organization by sending them to childcare centres in the Vanni" (p. 359), the rebels' stronghold in the north.[43]

---

[42] In her book *The Will to Freedom*, Adele Balasingham notes that she attended many weddings among senior cadres during her time with the group.
[43] See also Thamizhini (2020).

Others report that, following the rescinding of the ban on marriage in the LTTE, "members of the opposite sex are nonetheless strongly encouraged to marry while actively participating in the nationalist movement" and that LTTE leadership believed that marriage within the organization could "inspire a greater sense of commitment to the LTTE cause" (Jordan and Denov, 2013: 51). The rebels' established minimum ages for marriage (twenty-three for women and twenty-nine for men) and "it was expected that at least one of the two had to have served for at least five years in the Movement" (Thamizhini, 2020: 81). Similar to women in the TPLF, one account of women's motivations for participating in the organization suggested that some women joined in order to avoid unwanted marriages (see Gowrinathan, 2021).

Part of the reason for the contentiousness of debates about marriage within the LTTE was the rebels' conceptualization of where women fit into their political project and the gender norms of the Tamil community. The Tamil Tigers considered women's liberation contingent on the success of their nationalist project. Brun (2008) notes that the "LTTE claims that women can only be liberated through joining the movement, and in this respect the LTTE empowers the women with the idea of militancy" (p. 409). Simultaneously, the Tamil Tigers also needed the support of the Tamil community to legitimize themselves as a valid representative of the community's interests. Stack-O'Connor (2007) observes that women's "inclusion allowed the LTTE to argue to its Tamil audience that it was fully representative of the Tamil nation and more enlightened than other Tamil forces" (p. 48). Such competition between Tamil armed groups not only prompted women's inclusion but also encouraged the LTTE to take a stance against the dowry marriage tradition in order to attract more female support (Stack-O'Connor, 2007).[44]

Thus, marriage was a fraught issue for the rebels because of the need to incorporate women in a way that would not alienate the Tamil population. The LTTE's marriage policies were designed with nationalist and respectability politics in mind. In this balancing act, gender equality and women's interests within the organization could receive short shrift. Stack-O'Connor (2007) observes that the LTTE's regulations made women "armed virgins," who were expected to perform masculinity without being afforded the same liberties as men. This double standard was enforced through strict regulations on rebel sexual relations. Those who engaged in sex outside of marriage could face harsh punishments (Thamizhini, 2020). Thamizhini (2020) notes that the LTTE executed three women in 1994 for the crime of having slept with non-LTTE men.

---

[44] Also discussed in Balasingham (2001).

The rebels dedicated significant efforts to tracking relationships, organizing celebrations, and issuing marriage certifications. Within the LTTE, once marriage was permitted there was reportedly a fairly well-institutionalized process by which members of the organization tied the knot. According to Jordan and Denov (2013), "an assembly of elders is responsible for arranging marriages between members. LTTE cadres who wish to get married go to the department and they organize a five-minute marriage ceremony. Once the couple is married, the movement provides them with their own private place to stay as husband and wife" (p. 51). Balasingham's autobiography notes the leader of the political wing was also expected to coordinate the organization's "functions, including the weddings" (Balasingham, 2001: 341). The endorsement of marriage by the rebels thus required the establishment of a process as well as the creation of special housing accommodations for married couples and became a concern for the leadership's top echelons. Though a potentially labor-intensive process, facilitating marriages may have led to greater acceptance of the rebels by the Tamil population as it placated widespread discomfort with unmarried women associating with men (Tambiah, 2005).

Al-Shabaab

For al-Shabaab "marriage is not just the God-ordained way of life but a tool for recruitment and advancing sociopolitical interests. The group promises male recruits enhanced access to wives and greater social mobility, including by abolishing customs that prevent men from minor clans from marrying women from larger or more prominent ones" (Crisis Group, 2019: n.p.). Al-Shabaab places a particular emphasis on women's roles as wives and mothers within the organization; these identities are not apolitical but rather seen as an important way of supporting the rebels and contributing to their political project.

The rebels have taken a variety of approaches to promoting marriage within its ranks, including both forced and voluntary marriages.[45] While some men affiliated with al-Shabaab have continued to marry the "normal" way (i.e., courting a girl and seeking her family's approval to get married in line with prevalent customs), others have benefited greatly from al-Shabaab's support overcoming the challenges of finding a partner or affording a wedding. As one former member noted, the group provided support "such as accommodation and furniture. Women who are in the group collect money so that men who want to marry can get support"; other defectors noted that al-Shabaab provided money

---

[45] There is debate over the extent to which the wives of al-Shabaab members can be considered 'members' of the organization (Stern, 2019).

and instructions to get married to members and that in some instances "al-Shabaab can bring a woman for you" (Stern, 2019: 21).[46]

While many women have been forced or coerced into marriage, the rebels' marriage policy has also been used to attract and retain female members. "Khadija" and Harley observe that "Women who are married to Al-Shabaab fighters lead a privileged existence both in terms of the quality of life that is accorded to them by the Al-Shabaab's Executive Council, especially in comparison to the civilian population living under Al-Shabaab's control, and also the freedoms they are allowed" (Khadija and Harley, 2018: 252).[47] Other studies underscore how women may join the group because of the affection they feel towards recruiters or partners (Badurdeen, 2020). We should not overlook the political and ideological resonance of marriage for some of al-Shabaab's voluntary female recruits; one study of female al-Shabaab returnees noted that "two women explained their motivations to be wives of martyrs and expressed their desire with regard to religious obligations of being true Muslims, and to provide their role as Muslim women to support the Muslim Ummah" (Badurdeen, 2020: 623). Furthermore, the rebels' interpretation of wife inheritance has also served to strengthen cohesion within the group: if a woman's husband dies or defects, she is married to another member of the rebel group (Donnelly, 2019). Thus, marrying a member of al-Shabaab is, in many ways, a commitment to the organization, not just the individual.

Yet the importance of women within the organization is not merely symbolic; wives in al-Shabaab are responsible for a variety of tasks in service of the organization. Stern notes that women have been involved in tax collection, outreach to civilians, and the recruitment of women to serve as wives of rebel group members (Stern, 2020). Furthermore, in al-Shabaab, certain types of women are granted the authority to run their own businesses – which then become a source of economic support to the armed group (Stern, 2021). In particular, 'Khadija' and Harley note that women are imbued with the task of raising the next generation of al-Shabaab fighters, imbuing them with the group's values (Khadija and Harley, 2019). While the gendered division of labor also speaks to the rebels' ideology and the process of social reproduction in the rebel group, it also has tangible implications for women's experience during war and the logistical capabilities of the organization.

The dynamics of conflict and the extent to which the rebels control territory also seem to exert an influence over al-Shabaab's marriage policies. A defector explained to a researcher that "When al-Shabaab captures a town, they marry

---

[46] Also discussed in Donnelly (2019).
[47] As Benstead and Van Lehman (2021) unpack, women from minority ethnic groups are much more likely to be married under conditions that more closely resemble sexual slavery.

women. They encourage the men in the group to marry women. When they are in the bush, they discourage marriage, because they are not in town, so they will not access basic needs. Older men can continue their marriages. They stop young men marrying when they are in the bush" (Stern, 2020: 21). This may be explained by the robust infrastructure (and associated logistical burden) the rebels require to implement their vision of marriage. Stern (2020) observes that "great efforts are made to keep marriages within the al-Shabaab movement stable" (p. 21). Al-Shabaab reportedly gives scheduled leave to fighters so that they can visit their spouses (Stern, 2020). Across the territory it governs, al-Shabaab's governors form committees made up of wives of high-ranking officers and other female supporters. According to Stern (2020), "Women in these committees are said to act as 'marital counsellors of sorts', working to keep unsettled marriages stable" (p. 21).[48] When these attempts are unsuccessful, al-Shabaab's courts can process divorces – which seem to be a fairly common occurrence within the group (Stern, 2020).

Part of the reason that the rebels are willing to incur these costs may also lie in the ways in which their system of marriage has bonded them to certain communities, facilitating their operations (Donnelly, 2019). One study notes that

> when compared to majority clans, Bantu girls are enslaved by Al-Shabaab fighters at younger ages on average than brides from majority clans and that they typically remain with their own families. Because intermarriage between majority clans and the Bantu is not allowed in Somali society, Al-Shabaab fighters ignore the children of the Bantu girls and women, whom they despise as a racially distinct minority with low social status. (Benstead and Van Lehman, 2021: 387)

Furthermore, while the rebels once used the prospect of marriage to attract foreign recruits, some Somali families objected to this practice – suggesting that this aspect of the rebels' approach to marriage threatened their relationship with the community (Crisis Group, 2019). Thus, al-Shabaab's marriage policies furthered its efforts to broker ties with influential clans and reinforced prevailing discriminatory systems.

The Islamic State

Similar to al-Shabaab, the Islamic State relies on marriage as a means of actualizing its ideologically ordained position for women, which emphasizes their roles in the domestic realm. A piece of Islamic State propaganda, titled "Women in the Islamic State: Manifesto and Case Study," declares that "woman

---

[48] Rebels' management of marriage thus provides an avenue through which women affiliated with the organization can access power.

was created to populate the Earth just as man was. But, as God wanted it to be, she was made from Adam and for Adam. Beyond this, her creator ruled that there was no responsibility greater for her than that of being a wife to her husband" (Winter, 2015: 16). As Speckhard and Ellenberg (2020) note,

> marriage and motherhood were highly encouraged, if not outright mandated, for ISIS women. Women who arrived unmarried or who were widowed were not allowed to live as single women, and were generally forced to live in a women's guest house, what ISIS referred to as a *madhafa*. Conditions in the *madhafas* were so bad that single women and widows who otherwise would not remarry, frequently agreed to marriage simply to escape from them. (p. 107)

Marriage and the maintenance of separate spheres for men and women are important parts of the rebels' political project.

While the women enslaved by the Islamic State or forcibly married to members are obviously not integrated into the rebellion willingly, some women have been drawn to the Islamic State because of the rebels' policies regarding marriage. Many of the portrayals of the women who join the Islamic State and marry fighters tout unhelpful and sensationalistic depictions of these women as dumb or demonic "jihadi brides." Loken and Zelenz's work underscores that such portrayals are off base; they assert that "this devotion appears ultimately rooted in a gendered religious and political ideology – not the want for romantic affection" (Loken and Zelenz, 2016: 58). The Islamic State has been able to recruit and retain both male and female members on the basis of allowing them the ability to actualize a specific vision of marriage – though some eventually become disillusioned with the organization and its practice of marriage. Underscoring the importance of marriage to the Islamic State's cohesion and the centrality of it to its operations are reports that the widows of Islamic State fighters "were pressured to remarry immediately after their husbands' death, contravening Islamic prescriptions for three months of celibacy for widows" (Ahram, 2018: 188). Again, we see how reinterpretations of marriage practices are used to retain members of the organization.

Though the Islamic State articulates and enforces relatively traditional gender norms in its model of marriage, it has also endorsed "mixed-nationality and mixed-ethnicity marriages" (Trisko Darden and Hassan, 2023: 3). According to Trisko Darden and Hassan (2023) this reflects "the group's transnational nature and supranational political agenda" (p. 3). Ahram (2018) describes the Islamic State's policies regarding sexual violence and forced marriage as a form of state-building that continues, in many ways, preexisting patterns in its areas of operations. He observes that "arranged and enforced marriages fleshed out ISIS as a familial state in a different way, creating intra-Sunni bonds" (Ahram, 2018: 187), in addition to "augmenting its demographic base" (Ahram, 2018: 188).

Though novel in certain ways, he underscores that "ISIS's practices of sexual violence carried forward the prior repertoires of state-building in Syria and Iraq," noting, for example, that "Widows and families of martyrs received pensions, just as they had under Assad and Saddam" (Ahram, 2018: 187–188).

Though the rebels expend considerable energy in managing marriages within their ranks, these unions bolster their logistical capacity. Women play important logistical roles in the Islamic State in their roles as wives. Ahram (2018) notes that "in the same way that war-making stimulated the formation of the Syrian and Iraqi welfare system, the ISIS bureaucracy was attuned to the importance of marriage and family bonds to their state-building efforts" (p. 188). Furthermore, the Islamic State's efforts to raise the next generation of fighters is a burden that rests heavily on the shoulders of their mothers, the wives of Islamic State's fighters. As Spencer (2016) notes, "in ISIS ideology, the home symbolizes a woman's paradise ... Women are directed to continue religious studies while nurturing, educating, and protecting children from the influences of infidels. Unquestionably, a woman's greatest responsibility is to foster the next generation of jihad – a generation knowledgeable in Allah's ultimate destiny" (p. 82). Not only does the Islamic State depend on women's logistical contributions but the rebellion itself provides services and care to its members on the basis of their marital status and their dependents.[49]

While many of these unions are the site of abuse, coercion, and mistreatment, there are also some reports of genuine affection developing between husband and wife. Moaveni (2019) relays the account of Aws, whose Islamic State husband "Abu Mohammed liked to trace the two moles that made a constellation on her left cheek; he teased her about her accent when she tried to pronounced Turkish words" (p. 169); Moaveni notes that Aws "disliked his absences and would pout upon his return, and he would have to make silly jokes and cajole her into forgiving him" (p. 169). No such playfulness or care developed with her second husband after she was widowed by Abu Mohammed. Moaveni also recounts another woman, Dua, who cared deeply for her husband because he "had transformed her life completely" (p. 173) and who was "devastated" (p. 180) when he undertook a martyrdom operation.

Conclusions

The cozy conversation with Mariam and Fikru in their lovely home, both so familiar in tone and so new in context to me, encouraged me to consider the relevance of and variation within rebels' approaches to marriage. This section

---

[49] See, for example, an ISIS questionnaire and marriage contract: https://isisfiles.gwu.edu/down loads/zc77sq117?locale=en.

has, through available qualitative information on five non-state armed groups, revealed that the systems of rebel marriage reflect not only rebels' political project but also how rebel leadership weights the manner in which marriage may bolster or undermine internal cohesion and the logistical operations of the non-state armed group. When deciding how to approach marriage (and whether to change their current approach), rebels balance the relative costs and benefits of marriage as they relate to their logistical capabilities. Neither permitting nor banning marriage is costless; the emotional and romantic lives of rebels are yet another feature of member life that rebel leaders must provide for. More research is needed to understand if and when certain considerations outweigh others or if there are certain universal preconditions for rebels to allow marriage. This analysis has not uncovered any necessary conditions for rebels to allow marriage, though it has described a possible relationship between territorial control, logistical capabilities, and permitting marriage.

Ultimately, this section aims to catalyze greater and more systematic research into marriage in rebel groups as part of the literature's broader turn towards understanding the quotidian processes and experiences within rebel groups. It is not a comprehensive treatment of rebel marriage policies. The section introduces a framework for understanding how rebel groups approach the issue of marriage and discusses how these regulations affect women's lives during war, with the hope of spurring further comparative research on the subject. Marriages that take place among rebels during war do not necessarily end once the guns are silenced; furthermore, whether these unions persist into the post-conflict period or dissolve, the characteristics of wartime marriage systems can shape women's prospects for post-conflict reintegration. The following section considers the post-conflict legacies of rebel marriages, paying particular attention to how these wartime unions affect women's lives after war.

'Til Death Do Us Part: The Post-Conflict Legacies of Rebel Marriages

To build a revolution and to build a family are creative projects oriented towards the future.

(Matarazzo and Baines, 2019: 286)

We female fighters dreamed of bending the sky to a bow once. Now, all our dreams are dissolved, and we lie fallen at the threshold of reality.

(Thamizhini, 2020: 75)

As we have seen, there are important differences in the characteristics of rebel marriages during war, reflecting deliberations and priorities at the organizational level.[50] Though rebel marriages exhibit important variations, they often exercise a powerful influence over women's lives after war. While the site of deeply personal affairs, marriage also derives a degree of its gravity by formalizing a relationship in the eyes of others. Thus, the implications of these relationships extend beyond the dyadic relationship between husband and wife, affecting women's relations with their extended family, fellow community members, and representatives of the international community. In this section, I use evidence from the same five rebel groups discussed in Section 3 to introduce 'the other DDR'. This phrase refers to the non-mutually exclusive frames of depoliticization, distrust, and reclamation (DDR) that rebel marriages and rebel wives are often understood through in the post-conflict era or once they leave the group. I describe this as 'the other DDR' in reference to disarmament, demobilization, and reintegration (DDR) programs that often are instituted in post-conflict contexts. Such programs are a common feature of post-conflict settlements, particularly since the 1990s (Schulhofer-Wohl and Sambanis, 2020). These programs are aimed at preventing the recurrence of conflict by facilitating the return of combatants to civilian life (Schulhofer-Wohl and Sambanis, 2020). It has been difficult to assess the effectiveness of these formal DDR programs, despite their prominence and the frequency with which they receive international support (Muggah, 2005; Schulhofer-Wohl and Sambanis, 2020). Over the past three decades, there have been myriad approaches to these sorts of DDR programs, each attempting to learn from previous programs. However, important blind spots remain in the development and operationalization of these programs, which can disadvantage women associated with armed groups.

The STORM framework presented in the previous section can help us understand which of these narrative frames for understanding rebel wives and wartime marriages might be most prevalent. Of course, it is difficult to untangle the discrimination that female ex-rebels face by dint of their contributions to rebellion from the particular reception they receive because of their wartime marriage. The marginalization of women from DDR programs in general, the unevenness and unreliability of data collection on excombatants' marital states, and the difficulty in collecting reintegration data in general all limit the extent to which we can disaggregate the experiences of unmarried female rebels from their married peers. The literature that *has* examined this subject underscores

---

[50] Though this Element has not focused on forced marriages, perhaps the most consequential feature of rebel marriage is whether they are forced or voluntary; in the case of the former, they represent a profound violation of human rights that cannot be ignored. Rebel marriages also differ with respect to whether they are radical reinterpretations of existing marital practices or in line with them and whether they prove to be durable or ephemeral.

the deleterious consequences that misunderstandings of the dynamics of war-time marriages and their implications for women's lives after war have for female ex-rebels.

As the international community seeks to integrate gender-sensitivity into its policies and programs, there are some signs that the clunky and depoliticizing approaches that previous DDR programs took to wartime marriages may fall by the wayside. Indeed, guidance for military practitioners involved in DDR processes released in 2021 notes that "for female veterans, individual interviews are needed to determine whether they are in forced marriages, were impressed as sex slaves, and/or have children as a result. The pertinent question for 'married' females is whether they wish to separate from their alleged husbands" (Millen and Seligsohn, 2021: 70). The guidance further observes that female veterans may face difficulties remarrying in their communities of origin and note that wartime marriage patterns can influence which communities women choose to settle or resettle in (Millen and Seligsohn, 2021). The need to reserve physical space for families, distinct from the quarters of "single adult males, adult females, male child soldiers, [and] female child soldiers" in a cantonment, also reflects a more gender-sensitive approach to DDR that recognizes how wartime marriage practices can shape post-conflict needs (Millen and Seligsohn, 2021). However, the political significance of wives and wartime marriages often remains underappreciated and subject to erasure and misunderstanding in the postwar period.

Despite these challenges, it is still possible to leverage the STORM framework to predict how rebels' management of marriage may impact community reception. Because these three narratives are non-mutually exclusive, it is not possible to trace decisions about rebel marriages to *only* one outcome. Rather, we can consider how rebel marriage policies, the individual characteristics of rebel wives, and the overall conflict context interact to evoke a mixture of these three reactions. For example, depoliticization may be a way to rewrite women's wartime contributions to conform to prevalent gender norms, or it may reflect the ways in which the rebels' marriage practices reflect prevalent practices. When rebels reinterpret marriage customs in gender-egalitarian ways, these unorthodox marriage practices may result in the distrust of former rebel women or provoke efforts to reclaim these women. When rebel groups are still active and constitute a threat, even women in marriages with a fairly traditional division of labor may still be subject to distrust. The STORM framework, in conjunction with broader feminist conflict analysis, can thus help us identify possible obstacles and opportunities that former rebel women face as a result of their wartime marriages, both as a demographic category and at the individual level.

By taking seriously the dynamics of rebel marriage during wartime, we can better understand the social and economic landscape that former rebel women navigate after war. Importantly, however, it is difficult to untangle what stigma and mistrust that such women face are a result of rebel marriage policies and what comes from participation in a rebel group more generally. Rather than flattening these complexities, this section explores the myriad ways in which rebel marriage systems can affect women's lives after war – for better or for worse, in sickness and in health.

Depoliticization

Depoliticization of rebel wives involves subsuming their other roles in the organization to their identity as a wife, which is then rendered a marginal player in political violence. Narratives of depoliticization may suggest that women were duped into their position in the group, depriving them of their agency during war. Such a dynamic can manifest through disarmament, demobilization, and reintegration (DDR) programs that require a weapon to qualify or which provide benefits only to male members of the organization. In relegating such women's work to that of being 'just a wife', this approach fails to appreciate the myriad contributions that married female rebels provide. One report hypothesized that

> the reason for not working actively to include girls and women in institutionalized DDR programmes could be that female fighters also perform additional roles – they are labourers, 'wives', girlfriends, domestic workers, farmers – and this can render the notion of who is a fighter and who is not unclear. They are frequently represented, incorrectly, as being only dependants or wives of male fighters, and few efforts are made to determine whether in fact they were also fighters. (Coulter, Persson, and Utas, 2008: 22)

Prioritizing an ex-rebel's identity as a 'wife' to the extent that it overrides their other identities can contribute to depoliticization.

Community members in conflict-affected countries can also depoliticize former rebel wives; one report noted that research in Jubaland, Somalia found that many "were pragmatic and sympathetic around returning women" who left al-Shabaab, "noting that they presented *little threat as most were wives*" (Stern and Peterson, 2022: 22; emphasis added). Depoliticization ignores or brushes off the ways in which marriage – even while maintaining traditional gendered divisions of labor – can take on an especially resonant political salience during war.

Depoliticization can also occur when policies designed to enable women's reintegration as wives and mothers end up excluding them from benefits or prestige that other ex-rebels receive. In Nepal, for example, efforts to ensure that female combatants affiliated with the Maoists were included in DDR programming stumbled over the issues of marriage, childbirth, and childcare. This program was marked by a particularly long period of demobilization in cantonments and camps (Khadka, 2012). At least during the initial period of demobilization, wartime practices related to gender norms and the division of labor were continued; Bleie (2012) notes that "not only both sexes do the same demanding daily exercises; they shared similar duties in the canteens and living quarters. Even football matches were played together" (p. 12). As more members got married and became pregnant, however, the movement's revolutionary gender egalitarianism began to fray at the seams. As Hauge (2019) notes,

> When women became pregnant in the cantonments, the Maoist leadership opted for a scheme of three years of maternity leave, giving female combatants the right to retain their monthly allowance when on leave. This was an option that left the women very much on their own with responsibility for the child, without any kind of daycare arrangement or any involvement from male combatants. The consequence of this was that while senior female officers stayed with their families, the younger female officers moved to communities outside of the cantonments. The long period of leave often had the effect of seriously diminishing the rank mobility of female combatants as compared to their male counterparts. (p. 211)[51]

Thus, an ostensibly woman-friendly maternal leave policy, adopted by a leftist rebel group with a significant number of female members, backfired and resulted in women's marginalization.[52] The rebels' wartime efforts to make sure that being a wife or mother did not overrun women's identities as rebels were undermined after war.

Distrust

Distrust can manifest in many ways and to various degrees. For example, this narrative is employed when the wartime marriages are understood *only* through the lens of marriage as a potential human rights abuse, when those who are married within a rebel group are rendered as monstrous and undeserving of the state's or community's support *because* of their identity as a rebel wife,[53] and when the models of wartime marriage become suspect or undesirable in the postwar period.[54]

---

[51] Drawing on Bleie (2012).

[52] As a woman living in America, I had to read the "three years of [paid] maternity leave" multiple times before it fully sunk in that a demobilizing rebel group offered a more humane maternity leave policy than the richest country in the world.

[53] A continuation of the narrative of "Monster" articulated by Sjoberg and Gentry.

[54] It is also worth noting that former rebel women may face stigma because of their history of relationships within rebel groups that were *not* formalized as marriages. Consider, for example,

Stern and Peterson note that women formerly affiliated with al-Shabaab often face profound marginalization and ostracization from their communities. They note that once women defect from the group,

> many do not reveal that they were associated with al-Shabaab, as doing so might attract mistrust, stigma or even arrest. Many live quite isolated lives, cut off from communities, for fear of people finding out who they were. Where women's backgrounds are known, some are stigmatised and discriminated against – with some even rejected by their families due to their affiliation with the group. (Stern and Peterson, 2022: 13)

They further note that their marriages to al-Shabaab members can place them at risk for retaliation from the group, observing that "this is particularly the case when women flee with children, whom the group wishes to recruit" (Stern and Peterson, 2022: 14). Other reports note that it is not only the wives of al-Shabaab members that are subject to stigma from members of the community but also widows and children of fighters (Salifu, Ndung'u, and Sigsworth, 2017).

The wives of Islamic State fighters have also been subject to profound distrust and marginalization by members of the communities they are attempting to return to. A randomized study that asked about willingness to accept individuals formerly affiliated with the Islamic State found that

> respondents are least likely to allow the reintegration of collaborators who were physically closest to the Islamic State (those who worked as cooks for fighters) and those with family ties (wives of fighters) in contrast with collaborators in civilian roles who were working for institutions that provided services to other civilians (janitors working in the Islamic State's department of municipal services). (Revkin and Kao, 2020: 37)

Part of the reason for such high rates of rejection may be that 84 percent of respondents believed that being the wife of an Islamic State fighter was 'voluntary' (Revkin and Kao, 2020).[55]

Recently, distrust of wartime marriages among rebels has manifested as states stripping the citizenship rights of women on the basis of their marriage to

---

women formerly associated with the FARC who face trouble reintegrating into Colombian society because of such perceptions. As one review noted, "their suspected sexual promiscuity – or the belief that they may have suffered sexual violence – makes it more difficult for them to find partners, get married, and raise a family. Their reintegration into civilian life often requires them to accept roles that are traditionally assigned to women and often favoured by familial expectations and indeed public policies" (Boutron and Cuervo Gómez, 2017).

[55] In appeals to countries to repatriate women from their countries who had joined the Islamic State, UN representatives not only have argued about the legality of rendering someone stateless but have also asserted that these women were "groomed online." In this way, we see potential connections between whether women are depoliticized or distrusted (Nebehay, 2021).

Islamic State militants. Though it is a mistake to depoliticize marriage within non-state armed groups and women can play an important role in supporting rebel objectives and activities in their roles as wives, stripping women of their citizenship rather than using existing domestic legal institutions to hold them accountable is a troubling development (Benton and Banulescu-Bogdan, 2019). Citizenship revocation renders women and children stateless (Diaz, 2021).[56] This approach to rebel marriages implies that wives are irredeemable by dint of their relationships and thus they are owed nothing by the state. Further complicating the lives of women married to Islamic State fighters, according to Darden and Hassan, "The lack of clear marriage, divorce, and birth records for Islamic State affiliates and their children complicates efforts to establish the paternity of children and raises questions about whether these marriages are considered formal or informal by states" (Trisko Darden, and Hassan, 2023: 8). These deliberations have implications for the citizenship of any children born of these marriages and who bears legal responsibility for caring for these children (Trisko Darden, and Hassan, 2023). Distrust of rebel wives thus has tangible ramifications for women once they leave the group, including abandonment by their countries of origin and residence.

Distrust may also be likely to manifest when wartime marriages were reinterpreted by rebel groups to be in line with their revolutionary political project. Consider, for example, women in the CPN-M, who were encouraged to marry outside of their ethnicity and cast as members of the rebel group and who were socialized into the group's gender-egalitarian ideology. At the close of the conflict, their marriages to fellow rebels were double-edged swords. A number of women married to fellow ex-combatants "felt empowerment through their marriages, forming life alliances with men who support changed gender roles and hence are more appropriate partners for them" (K. C. and Van Der Haar, 2018: 448). The reinterpretation of marriage during war can become an important feature of women's identities. As Upreti and Shivakoti (2018) noted, "society did not easily (and wholeheartedly) accept [intercaste and interethnic marriages]" and that "in many cases even their parents and relatives did not accept such marriages" (p. 84). However encouraged these unions were during war, they were not widely accepted among the broader civilian population at the close of the conflict. Furthermore, the reassertion of prewar norms made it even more difficult to maintain the egalitarian and revolutionary character of wartime marriages; Yami (2021) notes that during war "a combined kitchen mess freed women from domestic duties," whereas "during the peace

---

[56] Human rights advocates have condemned the decision to strip women of their citizenship and are instead advocating that those suspected of supporting the Islamic State be formally tried.

period, women leaders had to again take on the burden of the kitchen and other household tasks besides their political work" (p. 247). This is not a dynamic unique to Nepal. Mariam, the TPLF veteran whose story opened this Element, told me that fighters' families were often confused by the dynamics of their wartime marriages as they persisted into the post-conflict period; with her typical candor, she told me that, back then, "our mothers really wonder about our marriages – we were running here and there for meetings".[57]

Distrust of wartime unions can also manifest *within* the marriage, prompting one or both partners to seek a separation. There is evidence across a number of cases that many female rebels become divorcees after war. One female veteran of the TPLF noted that, with the end of the war, male veterans had more "opportunities" relative to their time in the largely male rebellion, prompting many of them to leave their wartime spouse.[58] One study suggested that 60 percent of these "bush marriages" ended in divorce (Ababe, 2006). Similarly, in Nepal, the All Nepal Women's Union recorded 700 cases in which men left their wives after the war (Sthapit and Doneys, 2017: 45). According to Upreti and Shivakoti (2018), "many" of the unions between members of different castes "end up broken, and the female ex-combatants have to raise children alone, managing livelihoods as single mothers" (p. 83).

Thus, the distrust of wartime marriages and rebel wives can have profound implications for women's lives after war. Distrust can affect women's citizenship, economic and political status, well-being in the home, and their acceptance in the community. In post-conflict contexts, there is contestation and disagreement over what the economic, political, and social dynamics of society should look like. For many female ex-combatants who were married or romantically partnered during war, their home lives can become the front line in the fight over the proper roles for men and women. The models of wartime marriage that were present in the rebel group can become distrusted after war.

Reclamation

Reclaiming rebel wives involves rationalizing, legalizing, or otherwise accepting rebel wives for (or in spite of) their wartime marriage. Formalizing and recognizing wartime marriages is a formal manner by which the state can reassert its role as the arbiter of marriage and other social institutions in the aftermath of political violence, reclaiming female rebels as members of the community that they govern. For example, the Commissioner General of

---

[57] Mariam (Respondent 26).
[58] Respondent 33 and asserted by Mariam (Respondent 26) in author fieldwork.

Rehabilitation during the reintegration of LTTE combatants told journalists "it's only fair we legalise their marriages as part of their rehabilitation process," since many of the couples had children and had been in relationships (Hindustan Times, 2010). In her memoir, Thamizhini (a high-ranking woman in the LTTE) recalls a marriage arranged in her rehabilitation camp between two former fighters; she suggests that the wedding ceremony was necessary because "it was custom to release someone into the care of their families or close relatives after their rehabilitation was over" and the bride had no such family to claim her. By getting married, she could be released into the care of her in-laws. While this is presented to some degree as a heartwarming example of post-conflict reintegration, it also suggests that the postwar period was one in which former female fighters were not trusted to be their own keepers (Thamizhini, 2020: 187). This represents the reassertion of different authorities over women's lives. Furthermore, because the wedding was organized within a state-affiliated venue, it imbued the state with a degree of responsibility for allowing this young woman to return to normalcy. Reinstating state control over 'legitimate' marriage may represent an important part of returning 'to normal' after war, a manner of wresting social control away from armed groups, and a way of repudiating wartime reinterpretations of marriage.

Reclamation can also occur through efforts to teach former rebel women (and wives) how to perform appropriate femininity. In Sri Lanka, for example, "the rehabilitation programmes are re-feminising and re-domesticating ex-combatant women" (McFeeters, 2021: 297). Hills and MacKenzie (2017) observe that this is not an isolated case, writing that

> a common trend in these [DDR] training programmes is to offer men stereo-typically 'masculine' trades such as carpentry, masonry and works projects. Women, conversely, often receive training in areas of 'supplementary' income-generating activities, including soap-making, tie-dying, sewing and other 'feminized' roles . . . The types of skills offered to men tend to result in more stable and higher paid roles, while the skills targeted to women are often low paying or unpaid and less stable and valued. (p. 461)

Such a project design reflects an implicit assumption that women will not be breadwinners and reifies a traditional gendered division of labor. These skill-development programs can be in contravention of or in line with the gendered division of labor in wartime marriages; gender-normative job training may take on heightened importance, however, when women engaged in gender-transgressive activities during the war or when rebel marriage systems employ new gendered divisions of labor.

In some instances, the continuation and legitimization of wartime marriages can offer female ex-combatants social prestige and economic security. In Ethiopia, Azeb Mesfin's marriage to Meles Zenawi (an ideological pillar of the TPLF as both a rebel group and a political party, who served as Prime Minister from 1995 until his death in 2012) facilitated her rise to influential positions in the nation's economy and election to the country's legislature; the two met while rebels within the TPLF. Similarly, Hisila Yami's marriage to Baburam Bhattarai and the continuation of their relationship through the CPN-M's struggle and postwar period affected her influence within the party and, ultimately, put her in a position of power as the country's first lady during Bhattarai's tenure as prime minister (Yami, 2021). Without undermining the agency and capabilities of these women, it is important to consider how the legitimization of wartime marriages can secure certain women's positions in elite circles. Notably, both the TPLF and the CPN-M went on to be influential political parties, suggesting that this form of reclamation may not be available to rebel wives in groups that did not undergo such a transition.

Reclamation may also take the form of institutionalizing some of the wartime marriage practices of the rebels. Consider, for example, that postwar Tigray regional state passed the Family Law, which reflected some of the TPLF's wartime marriage regulations like prohibitions on child marriage; this state-level reform served as a template for national family law reform, which followed several years later.[59] As one women's rights activist told me, female Tigrayan activists were influential in pushing this postwar reform; she characterized these activists as asserting "we will not have less than in the bush."[60] Again, this sort of reclamation may be predicated on the outcome of the conflict and rate of the rebellion.

Conclusions

This section introduces a three-pronged framework for understanding how rebel wives are received after war; I suggest that former rebel wives and rebel marriages face depoliticization, distrust, and reclamation (DDR) after war. I highlight how the STORM framework introduced previously can help us understand which of these frames may be most prevalent after war, based on how rebels practiced marriage during war. Furthermore, this section unpacks how the durability or dissolution of wartime marriages affects women's lives after war. This discussion emphasizes that the politics of marriage do not remain within the confines of the home.

---

[59] Respondent 36 in author fieldwork.   [60] Respondent 4 in author fieldwork.

Conclusions and Avenues for Future Research

No union is more profound than marriage, for it embodies the highest ideals of love, fidelity, devotion, sacrifice, and family. In forming a marital union, two people become something greater than once they were.[61]

Summary and Conclusions

I still keep in touch with Mariam, the TPLF veteran who met and married Fikru during their time fighting the Ethiopian government, periodically. When her husband passed away, I called to offer my condolences. It felt impossible to me that a love that had been so remarkable – almost mythological in my mind – could end in something as mundane as widowhood. That is perhaps one of the most intoxicating parts of thinking about marriage during war: it is a way of observing exceptional events through the lens of a common experience. By comparing rebel marriage with civilian practices, we can gain a clearer understanding of how rebel groups operate and the quotidian experiences of rebels themselves.

A burgeoning literature suggests that the quotidian experiences of rebels – who they love, the clothes they wear (Parkinson, 2020), the food they eat, and even where they relieve themselves (Gutiérrez D, 2021) – should be taken as seriously as matters like rebel ideology, troop numbers, and rebel leadership. Given that rebel groups are often seeking to overturn the prevailing social and political order, it is perhaps unsurprising that they would exercise control over marriages of their members. As a part of taking a more holistic approach to understanding rebellion, we must also take seriously the 'feminine' or soft dynamics of rebel life that have been marginalized from traditional security studies. As this Element underscores, doing so will both provide a better understanding of women's lives within and after rebellion and imbue us with a deeper understanding of how rebel groups operate.

To further this line of research, this Element introduces the STORM framework. This framework sheds light on why rebel groups take different approaches to rebel marriage – and why rebel groups may change their approach to marriage over the course of the conflict. I suggest that rebels weigh the threats posed and opportunities presented by marriage, paying careful attention to how marriage relates to the rebels' political project, the anticipated effect on cohesion and retention, and the rebels' logistical capabilities. Applying this framework demonstrates that rebels often have to balance costs and benefits across these three categories; moreover, the framework highlights how rebels often allocate scarce resources and attention from high-ranking officials in managing rebel marriages. The STORM framework helps us understand the sometimes

---

[61] *Obergefell* v. *Hodges*, 576 U.S. 644 (2015), p. 28.

puzzling degree of consideration that rebels afford marriage and the group-specific reinterpretations of marriage practices. It is a valuable tool for those interested in rebel groups' internal practices and the experiences of female rebels during war.

Furthermore, the STORM framework can shed light on some of the challenges that female rebels often face after the war ends and they leave the rebel group. I introduce the concept of 'the other DDR', or the depoliticization, distrust, and reclamation that rebel wives and rebel marriages face after war. The STORM framework can help us anticipate which narrative may be more prevalent and what aspects of rebel marriage practices may provoke the employment of these frames – though there are no set trajectories based solely on wartime marriage practices. For example, when rebel marriage practices are distinctly out of line with civilian practices, distrust may be rife. When rebel marriages are in line with existing practices or gender relations, rebel marriages and rebel wives may be subject to depoliticization and reclamation. Rebel marriages and the frames through which they are understood after war shape the trajectory of former rebel women's lives and condition the dynamics of their reintegration.

By providing a comparative account of rebels' regulation of marriage during wartime and the post-conflict implications of these relationships, this Element is intended to spur further comparative research into rebel marriage systems and their implications for women's experiences during and after war.

Limitations of the Element and Future Research

While this Element contributes to our understanding of how non-state armed groups operate and the implications, the conditions of women's contribution to rebellion, and former rebel women's lives after war, it has several important limitations that offer compelling subjects for future study. Among the most obvious areas where additional research is needed are the issues of how pregnancy, childbirth, and childcare are managed in rebel groups. Much like marriage, these activities also reflect rebels' logistics, recruitment, and socio-political agenda – and exert an important influence over women's experiences during and after war. There is compelling evidence, from a variety of sources, that some rebel leaders devote considerable attention to childcare. For example, a number of accounts emphasize the amount of effort that the Islamic State places on raising the next generation of fighters (see Vale, 2019). It is well-known that the FARC made contraception mandatory and instituted policies that encouraged that encouraged female fighters who became pregnant to abort or to give their child to family members or civilians (Sanín and Carranza Franco, 2017). Those I spoke to about the TPLF's policies suggested that reforms related to marriage followed a degree of territorial control, enabling them to provide a safe place for mothers and children before allowing pregnancy and childbirth among members.[62] Hauge (2020) suggests that rebel policies requiring that rebels give up their children during war have "strong negative psychological consequences for both of the parents, although particularly for the mother"; her study also underlines the difficulties that parents face after war when trying to reunite with their children. She relays the account of a woman who became pregnant while serving with the FARC who followed rebel regulations and left her child with civilians; "after the peace agreement, she could not find her child, as no record had been kept and nobody now knew where her child was" (Hauge, 2020: 3). Other recent work underscores the ways in which fatherhood and marriage can affect men's commitment to rebellion and their postwar lives (Aijazi and Baines, 2017; Matarazzo and Baines, 2019). Future work can unpack the variation in these rebel group policies and the post-conflict implications of these practices.

Relatedly, this Element has not addressed how rebel groups obtain birth control and instruct members on the proper use of whatever contraceptives they procure. Both of these processes can provide invaluable insights into how rebel groups manage logistical supply chains and rebel socialization processes. Furthermore, discussions about how rebels manage contraception may also shed light on gendered power dynamics within rebel groups. One female veteran of the TPLF recalled that men resisted using condoms, even though that was the simplest form of birth control.[63]

Additionally, the Element has not discussed queer relationships in non-state armed groups and how non-state armed groups manage the issue of homosexuality. Rebel groups' approaches to homosexual relationships are not only important for the well-being of LGBTQIA+ communities in war zones but also can provide insights into the ideology and social objectives of the armed group (see Loken and Hagen, 2022).

Additional research is also needed to articulate men's experiences with wartime marriage and the post-conflict implications of these unions for men's economic, political, and social well-being. An emergent strand in the literature underscores that a forced marriage is a crime against the husband as well as the wife; future research can investigate how men relate to their wartime identities as husbands during and after conflict (see Matarazzo and Baines, 2019; Denov and Drumbl, 2020; Suarez and Baines, 2021). As this Element identified in the Introduction, marriage is a dyadic process – how marriage shapes men's

---

[62] Respondent 7 (who is also Fikru) was explicit about this, while others described this reform as taking place in the mid-to-late 1980s, after a significant shift in conflict dynamics.
[63] Respondent 26 in author fieldwork.

experiences during war, how it intersects with wartime masculinities, and how it conditions men's post-conflict opportunities are all worthy areas of future study.

Further research should be conducted to understand gaps that may exist between rebel groups' formal policies regarding marriage and their actual practices of marriage (Wood, 2018). Relatedly, this Element has not interrogated in any great detail differences among different ranks or units within the same rebel group. In especially decentralized rebel groups, for example, one might expect a greater degree of heterogeneity with respect to marriage regulations and experiences. Furthermore, a rebel's ability to marry and the characteristics of that marriage may depend on their position in the rebel hierarchy.

In taking marriage seriously in the study of war and rebel operations, we have the opportunity to understand a new set of bonds and regulations that hold sway over rebels' lives during and after war. It is my profound hope that this Element inspires further interrogation of the nature of being in love and at war.

References

Ababe, S. (2006). Ethiopian Women Return to Fight a New War. *ReliefWeb* [online]. https://reliefweb.int/report/ethiopia/ethiopian-women-return-fight-new-war.

Ahram, A. I. (2018). Sexual Violence, Competitive State Building, and Islamic State in Iraq and Syria. *Journal of Intervention and Statebuilding*, 13(2), pp. 180–196. https://doi.org/10.1080/17502977.2018.1541577.

Aijazi, O. and Baines, E. (2017). Relationality, Culpability and Consent in Wartime: Men's Experiences of Forced Marriage. *International Journal of Transitional Justice*, 11(3), pp. 463–483. https://doi.org/10.1093/ijtj/ijx023.

Annan, J., Blattman, C., Mazurana, D., and Carlson, K. (2009). Women and Girls at War: Wives, Mothers, and Fighters in the Lord's Resistance Army. Households in Conflict Network (HICN) Working Paper No. 63. www.hicn.org/wp-content/uploads/2012/06/wp63.pdf.

Asal, V., Avdan, N., and Shuaibi, N. (2020). Women Too: Explaining Gender Ideologies of Ethnopolitical Organizations. *Studies in Conflict and Terrorism*, 46(4), pp.1–18. https://doi.org/10.1080/1057610x.2020.1759256.

Badurdeen, F. A. (2020). Women Who Volunteer: A Relative Autonomy Perspective in al-Shabaab Female Recruitment in Kenya. *Critical Studies on Terrorism*, 13(4), pp. 616–637. https://doi.org/10.1080/17539153.2020.1810993.

Baines, E. (2014). Forced Marriage As a Political Project. *Journal of Peace Research*, 51(3), pp. 405–417. https://doi.org/10.1177/0022343313519666.

Balasingham, A. (2001). *The Will to Freedom: An Inside View of Tamil Resistance*. London: Fairmax.

Basham, V. M. and Catignani, S. (2018). War Is Where the Hearth Is: Gendered Labor and the Everyday Reproduction of the Geopolitical in the Army Reserves. *International Feminist Journal of Politics*, 20(2), pp. 153–171. https://doi.org/10.1080/14616742.2018.1442736.

Benstead, L. J. and Van Lehman, D. (2021). Two Classes of "Marriage": Race and Sexual Slavery in al-Shabaab-Controlled Somalia. *The Journal of the Middle East and Africa*, 12(4), pp. 385–403. https://doi.org/10.1080/21520844.2021.1923998.

Benton, M. and Banulescu-Bogdan, N. (2019). Foreign Fighters: Will Revoking Citizenship Mitigate the Threat? *Migration Policy Institute* [online], April 3. www.migrationpolicy.org/article/foreign-fighters-will-revoking-citizenship-mitigate-threat.

Berhe, M. G. (2018). From Left-Wing Liberation Army into a Government: The Challenges of Transition and the Case of TPLF/EPRDF. PhD dissertation, University of Victoria. http://dspace.library.uvic.ca/handle/1828/9427.

Bhaumik, S. (2002). Indian Rebels Ban Women. *BBC News* [online], November 29. http://news.bbc.co.uk/2/hi/south_asia/2528749.stm.

Bleie, T. (2012). *Post-War Moral Communities in Somalia and Nepal: Gendered Practices of Exclusion and Inclusion.* Tromsø: Center for Peace Studies at the University of Tromsø. https://uit.no/Content/307291/Post_War_Processes_ Report_Final.pdf.

Boutron, C. and Cuervo Gómez, D. (2017). From Rifles to Aprons? The Challenges of Reincorporating Colombia's Female Ex-combatants into Civilian and Political Life. LSE Latin American and Caribbean Center (online blog), March 8. https://blogs.lse.ac.uk/latamcaribbean/2017/03/08/ from-rifles-to-aprons-the-challenges-of-reincorporating-colombias-female- ex-combatants-into-civilian-and-political-life/.

Branstetter, R. W. (1983). Military Constraints upon Marriages of Services Members Overseas, or, If the Army Had Wanted You to Have a Wife. *Military Law Review*, 102, pp. 5–22.

Brathwaite, K. J. H. (2017). Boys Will Be Boys? The Normative Sources of Prostitution Policy in the German and American Militaries during World War II. *Journal of Global Security Studies*, 2(1), pp. 39–54. https://doi.org/ 10.1093/jogss/ogw023.

Brun, C. (2008). Birds of Freedom: Young People, the LTTE, and Representations of Gender, Nationalism, and Governance in Northern Sri Lanka. *Critical Asian Studies*, 40(3), pp. 399–422. https://doi.org/10.1080/ 14672710802274128.

Bunting, A., Tasker, H., and Lockhart, E. (2021). Women's Law-Making and Contestations of "Marriage" in African Conflict Situations. *Law and Society Review*, 55(4), pp. 614–633. https://doi.org/10.1111/lasr.12576.

Busari, S. and Jones, B. (2016). Escaped Chibok Girl: I Miss My Boko Haram Husband. *CNN* [online], August 16. https://edition.cnn.com/2016/08/16/ africa/chibok-girl-amina-ali-nkeki-boko-haram-husband/index.html#:~: text=Amina%20Ali%20Nkeki%2C%20her%20husband.

Campbell, J. (2018). Notorious Algerian Terrorist Mokhtar Belmokhtar Could Still Be Alive. Council on Foreign Relations [online blog]. www.cfr.org/blog/ notorious-algerian-terrorist-mokhtar-belmokhtar-could-still-be-alive#:~: text=Notorious%20Algerian%20Terrorist%20Mokhtar%20Belmokhtar% 20Could%20Still%20Be%20Alive.

Carlson, K. and Mazurana, D. (2008). *Forced Marriage within the Lord's Resistance Army, Uganda.* Boston, MA: Feinstein International Center.

https://fic.tufts.edu/publication-item/forced-marriage-with-the-lords-resist ance-army-uganda/.

Celello, K. and Kholoussy, H. (2016). Introduction: Global Perspectives on Marriage, Crisis, and Nation. In K. Celello and H. Kholoussy (eds.), *Domestic Tensions, National Anxieties: Global Perspectives on Marriage, Crisis, and Nation*. New York: Oxford University Press, pp. 1–15.

Cornelius, C. and Monk-Turner, E. (2019). I'll Trade You Skittles for a Blowjob: Assessing the Role of Anti-female Memes in Military Sexual Harassment and Assault. *Journal of Political and Military Sociology*, 46(1), pp. 221–260. www.jstor.org/stable/48599462.

Coulter, C. (2009). *Bush Wives and Girl Soldiers: Women's Lives through War and Peace in Sierra Leone*. Ithaca, NY: Cornell University Press.

Coulter, C., Persson, M., and Utas, M. (2008). *Young Female Fighters in African Wars: Conflict and Its Consequences*. The Nordic Africa Institute Policy Dialogue No. 3. Uppsala: The Nordic Africa Institute. www.diva-portal.org/smash/get/diva2:850362/FULLTEXT01.pdf.

Crisis Group (2019). Women and al-Shabaab's Insurgency. International Crisis Group Briefing No. 145, June 27. www.crisisgroup.org/africa/horn-africa/somalia/b145-women-and-al-shabaabs-insurgency.

Denov, M. S. and Drumbl, M. A. (2020). The Many Harms of Forced Marriage. *Journal of International Criminal Justice*, 18(2), pp. 349–372. https://doi .org/10.1093/jicj/mqaa007.

Diaz, J. (2021). No Country Will Take Them: Alleged ISIS Widow with Kids the Latest of Many in Limbo. *NPR* [online], March 26. www.npr.org/2021/ 03/26/975149256/no-country-will-take-them-alleged-isis-widow-with-kids-the-latest-of-many-in-lim.

Donnelly, P. (2018). The Interactive Relationship between Gender and Strategy. *Global Society*, 32(4), pp. 457–476. https://doi.org/10.1080/13600826 .2018.1490252.

Donnelly, P. (2019). Wedded to Warfare: Forced Marriage in Rebel Groups. PhD thesis, Tufts University.

Donnelly, P. and Myers, E. (2023). *Forced Marriage by Non-state Armed Groups: Frequency, Forms, and Impact*. International Peace Institute [online], April 17. www.ipinst.org/2023/04/forced-marriage-by-non-state-armed-groups-frequency-forms-and-impact.

Dubal, S. (2016). Rebel Kinship and Love within the Lord's Resistance Army. *Journal of Peace and Security Studies*, 2(1), pp. 20–32.

Enloe, C. (1980). Women: The Reserve Army of Army Labor. *Review of Radical Political Economics*, 12(2), pp. 42–52. https://doi.org/10.1177/ 048661348001200206.

Enloe, C. (2000). *Maneuvers: The International Politics of Militarizing Women's Lives*. Berkeley: University of California Press.

Enloe, C. (2016). Flick of the Skirt: A Feminist Challenge to IR's Coherent Narrative. *International Political Sociology*, 10(4), pp. 320–331. https://doi.org/10.1093/ips/olw017.

Estrada-Fuentes, M. (2016). Affective Labors: Love, Care, Solidarity in the Social Reintegration of Female Ex-combatants in Colombia. *Lateral*, 6(1). https://doi.org/10.25158/l5.2.10.

Fineman, M. A. (2001). Why Marriage? *Virginia Journal of Social Policy and the Law*, 9(1), pp. 239–272. https://heinonline.org/HOL/P?h=hein.journals/vajsplw9&i=249.

Florea, A. (2020). Rebel Governance in De Facto States. *European Journal of International Relations*, 26(4), pp. 1004–1031. https://doi.org/10.1177/1354066120919481.

Forney, J. F. (2015). Who Can We Trust with a Gun? Information Networks and Adverse Selection in Militia Recruitment. *Journal of Conflict Resolution*, 59(5), pp. 824–849. https://doi.org/10.1177/0022002715576752.

Gassmann, J. N. N. (2010). Patrolling the Homefront: The Emotional Labor of Army Wives Volunteering in Family Readiness Groups. PhD dissertation, University of Kansas. http://hdl.handle.net/1808/7420.

Gayer, L. (2012). Have Gun, Will Travel: Interpreting the Trajectories of Female Irregular Combatants. In Y. Guichaoua (ed.), *Understanding Collective Political Violence: Conflict, Inequality and Ethnicity*. London: Palgrave Macmillan, pp.105–123. https://doi.org/10.1057/9780230348318_6.

Gayer, L. (2013). "Love–Marriage–Sex" in the People's Liberation Army. In M. Lecomte-Tilouine (ed.), *Revolution in Nepal: An Anthropological and Historical Approach to the People's War*. Oxford: Oxford University Press, pp. 333–366. https://hal.science/hal-03393098/.

Gill, L. (1997). Creating Citizens, Making Men: The Military and Masculinity in Bolivia. *Cultural Anthropology*, 12(4), pp. 527–550. https://doi.org/10.1525/can.1997.12.4.527.

Giri, K. and Haer, R. (2021). Female Combatants and Durability of Civil War. *Studies in Conflict and Terrorism*, pp. 1–22. https://doi.org/10.1080/1057610x.2021.1980982.

Goodwin, J. (1997). The Libidinal Constitution of a High-Risk Social Movement: Affectual Ties and Solidarity in the Huk Rebellion, 1946 to 1954. *American Sociological Review*, 62(1), pp. 53–69. https://doi.org/10.2307/2657452.

Gowrinathan, N. (2021). *Radicalizing Her: Why Women Choose Violence.* Boston, MA: Beacon Press.

Gutiérrez D, J. A. (2021). Eating, Shitting and Shooting: A Scatological and Culinary Approximation to the Daily Lives of Rebels. *Studies in Conflict and Terrorism*, 46(10), pp. 1–38. https://doi.org/10.1080/1057610x.2021.1886432.

Gutiérrez-Sanín, F. (2018). The FARC's Militaristic Blueprint. *Small Wars and Insurgencies*, 29(4), pp. 629–653. https://doi.org/10.1080/09592318.2018.1497288.

Hammond, J. (1989). *Sweeter Than Honey: Ethiopian Women and Revolution.* Trenton, NJ: Red Sea Press.

Hammond, J. (1990). "My Revolution Is Like Honey": Women in Revolutionary Tigray. *Women: A Cultural Review*, 1(1), pp. 56–59. https://doi.org/10.1080/09574049008578021.

Hauge, W. I. (2019). Gender Dimensions of DDR – beyond Victimization and Dehumanization: Tracking the Thematic. *International Feminist Journal of Politics*, 22(2), pp. 206–226. https://doi.org/10.1080/14616742.2019.1673669.

Hauge, W. I. (2020). *Guerrilla Babies: Gender and Pregnancy Policies of Armed Groups.* Peace Research Institute Oslo Policy Brief No. 3 [online]. www.prio.org/publications/12647.

Heuveline, P. and Poch, B. (2006). Do Marriages Forget Their Past? Marital Stability in Post-Khmer Rouge Cambodia. *Demography*, 43(1), pp. 99–125. https://doi.org/10.1353/dem.2006.0005.

Hills, C. and MacKenzie, M. (2017). Women in Non-state Armed Groups after War: The (Non) Evolution of Disarmament, Demobilization and Reintegration. In R. Woodward and C. Duncanson (eds.), *The Palgrave International Handbook of Gender and the Military.* London: Palgrave Macmillan, pp. 455–471.

Hindustan Times. (2010). Sri Lanka Holds Mass Wedding for Ex-rebels. *Hindustan Times* [online], June 13. www.hindustantimes.com/world/sri-lanka-holds-mass-wedding-for-ex-rebels/story-URftQiMEgCWA4RTBro2uvN.html.

Huang, R. (2017). *The Wartime Origins of Democratization: Civil war, Rebel Governance, and Political Regimes.* Cambridge: Cambridge University Press.

Huang, R. and Sullivan, P. L. (2020). Arms for Education? External Support and Rebel Social Services. *Journal of Peace Research*, 58(4), pp. 794–808. https://doi.org/10.1177/0022343320940749.

Hudson, V. M. and Matfess, H. (2017). In Plain Sight: The Neglected Linkage between Brideprice and Violent Conflict. *International Security*, 42(1), pp. 7–40. https://doi.org/10.1162/isec_a_00289.

Hurl-Eamon, J. (2014). *Marriage and the British Army in the Long Eighteenth Century: 'The Girl I Left Behind Me'.* Oxford: Oxford University Press.

Hynd, S. (2016). "To Be Taken As a Wife Is a Form of Death": The Social, Military, and Humanitarian Dynamics of Forced Marriage and Girl Soldiers in African Conflicts, c.1990–2010. In A. Bunting, B. N. Lawrance, and R. L. Roberts (eds.), *Marriage by Force? Contestation over Consent and Coercion in Africa*. Athens: Ohio University Press, pp. 290–310 [online]. ore.exeter.ac.uk. http://hdl.handle.net/10871/32051.

Institute for War and Peace Reporting (2007). Uganda: Returning Rebel Women Face Rejection. *ReliefWeb* [online]. https://reliefweb.int/report/uganda/uganda-returning-rebel-women-face-rejection.

Jordan, K. and Denov, M. (2013). Birds of Freedom? Perspectives on Female Emancipation and Sri Lanka's Liberation Tigers of Tamil Eelam. *Journal of International Women's Studies*, 9(1). https://vc.bridgew.edu/jiws/vol9/iss1/3/.

K. C., L. and Van Der Haar, G. (2018). Living Maoist Gender Ideology: Experiences of Women Ex-combatants in Nepal. *International Feminist Journal of Politics*, 21(3), pp. 434–453. https://doi.org/10.1080/14616742.2018.1521296.

Khadija and Harley, S. (2019). Women in Al Shabaab. In M. Keating and M. Waldman (eds.), *War and Peace in Somalia: National Grievances, Local Conflict and Al-Shabaab*. Oxford: Oxford University Press, pp. 251–256 [online]. https://academic.oup.com/book/35091/chapter/299148942.

Khadka, S. (2012). Female Combatants and Ex-combatants in Maoist Revolution and Their Struggle for Reintegration in Post-War, Nepal. Master's thesis, The Arctic University of Norway. https://hdl.handle.net/10037/3980.

Kiconco, A. and Nthakomwa, M. (2018). Marriage for the "New Woman" from the Lord's Resistance Army: Experiences of Female Ex-abductees in Acholi Region of Uganda. *Women's Studies International Forum*, 68, pp. 65–74. https://doi.org/10.1016/j.wsif.2018.02.008.

Kime, P. (2020). Demand for Military Couples Counseling on the Rise, Officials Say. Military.com [online], October 30. www.military.com/daily-news/2020/10/30/demand-military-couples-counseling-rise-officials-say.html.

King, G., Keohane, R. O. and Verba, S. (2021). *Designing Social inquiry: Scientific Inference in Qualitative Research*. Princeton, NJ: Princeton University Press.

Kramer, S. A. (2012). Forced Marriage and the Absence of Gang Rape: Explaining Sexual Violence by the Lord's Resistance Army in Northern Uganda. *The Journal of Politics and Society*, 23(1), pp. 11–49. https://doi.org/10.7916/d8qc01g1.

Kroska, A. (2007). Gender Ideology and Gender Role Ideology. In G. Ritzer (ed.), *The Blackwell Encyclopedia of Sociology* [online]. https://doi.org/10.1002/9781405165518.wbeosg019.

Krystalli, R. and Schulz, P. (2022). Taking Love and Care Seriously: An Emergent Research Agenda for Remaking Worlds in the Wake of Violence. *International Studies Review*, 24(1). https://doi.org/10.1093/isr/viac003.

Kunz, R. and Sjoberg, A.-K. (2009). Empowered or Oppressed? Female Combatants in the Colombian Guerrilla: The Case of the Revolutionary Armed Forced of Colombia – FARC. *The Annual Convention of the International Studies Association*, pp.1–34.

Lanzona, V. A. (2009). *Amazons of the Huk Rebellion: Gender, Sex, and Revolution in the Philippines*. Madison: University of Wisconsin Press.

Lazarev, E. (2019). Laws in Conflict: Legacies of War, Gender, and Legal Pluralism in Chechnya. *World Politics*, 71(4), pp. 667–709. https://doi.org/10.1017/s0043887119000133.

LeVine, P. (2010). *Love and Dread in Cambodia*. Singapore: NUS Press.

Lie, J. (1997). The State As Pimp: Prostitution and the Patriarchal State in Japan in the 1940s. *The Sociological Quarterly*, 38(2), pp. 251–263. https://doi.org/10.1111/j.1533-8525.1997.tb00476.x.

Loken, M. (2022). Noncombat Participation in Rebellion: A Gendered Typology. *International Security*, 47(1), pp. 139–170. https://doi.org/10.1162/isec_a_00440.

Loken, M. (in press). *Women, Gender, and Rebel Governance in Civil Wars*. Elements in Gender and Politics. Cambridge: Cambridge University Press.

Loken, M. and Hagen, J. J. (2022). Queering Gender-Based Violence Scholarship: An Integrated Research Agenda. *International Studies Review*, 24(4).

Loken, M. and Matfess, H. (2023). Introducing the Women's Activities in Armed Rebellion (WAAR) Project, 1946–2015. *Journal of Peace Research*, p.002234332211283. https://doi.org/10.1177/00223433221128340.

Loken, M. and Zelenz, A. (2016). Explaining Extremism: Western Women in Daesh. *European Journal of International Security*, 3(1). https://doi.org/10.1017/eis.2017.13.

Loyle, C. E., Cunningham, K. G., Huang, R., and Jung, D. F. (2021). New Directions in Rebel Governance Research. *Perspectives on Politics*, 21(1), pp. 1–13. https://doi.org/10.1017/s1537592721001985.

Mampilly, Z. C. (2017). *Rebel Rulers: Insurgent Governance and Civilian Life during War*. Ithaca, NY: Cornell University Press.

Manivannan, Q., Anumol, D., Raja, S., et al. (2023). Care Conversations. *International Feminist Journal of Politics*, 25(2), pp. 336–352. https://doi.org/10.1080/14616742.2023.2190341.

Marks, Z. (2013). Sexual Violence inside Rebellion: Policies and Perspectives of the Revolutionary United Front of Sierra Leone. *Civil Wars*, 15(3), pp. 359–379. https://doi.org/10.1080/13698249.2013.842749.

Matarazzo, A. and Baines, E. (2019). Becoming Family: Futurity and the Soldier-Father. *Critical Military Studies*, 7(3), pp.1–18. https://doi.org/10.1080/23337486.2019.1631728.

Matfess, H. (in press). New Frontiers in Rebel Socialization: Considering Care and Marriage. *Civil Wars*.

McFeeters, A. (2021). Media Representations of Women Ex-combatants in Sri Lanka. In J. D. Brewer and A. Wahidin (eds.), *Ex-combatants' Voices: Transitioning from War to Peace in Northern Ireland, South Africa and Sri Lanka*. London: Palgrave Macmillan.

Mehreteab, A. (2002). Veteran Combatants Do Not Fade Away: A Comparative Study on Two Demobilization and Reintegration Exercises in Eritrea. Bonn International Centre for Conflict Studies Working Paper No. 23.

Mendez, A. (2012). Militarized Gender Performativity: Women and Demobilization in Colombia's FARC and AUC. PhD thesis, Queen's University.

Millen, R. and Seligsohn, N. (2021). *Disarmament, Demobilization, and Reintegration Programs for Military Practitioners*. Carlisle, PA: US Army Peacekeeping and Stability Operations Institute. https://pksoi.armywarcollege.edu/index.php/disarmament-demobilization-and-reintegration-programs-for-ilitary-practitioners/.

Ministere des Armées (n.d.). Life in a Regiment / Permissions and Family Life. *Légion étrangère* [online]. www.legion-recrute.com/en/life-regiment-permissions-and-family-life.

Moaveni, A. (2019). *Guest House for Young Widows: Among the Women of ISIS*. New York: Random House.

Moghadam, V. M. (1995). Gender and Revolutionary Transformation: Iran 1979 and East Central Europe 1989. *Gender and Society*, 9(3), pp. 328–358. https://doi.org/10.1177/089124395009003005.

Muggah, R. (2005). No Magic Bullet: A Critical Perspective on Disarmament, Demobilization and Reintegration (DDR) and Weapons Reduction in Post-conflict Contexts. *The Round Table*, 94(379), pp. 239–252. https://doi.org/10.1080/00358530500082684.

Nebehay, S. (2021). U.N. Urges 57 Countries to Reclaim Women, Children from Syrian Camps. *Reuters* [online], February 8. www.reuters.com/article/us-syria-security-un-rights-idUSKBN2A81V4.

Negewo–Oda, B. and White, A. M. (2011). Identity Transformation and Reintegration among Ethiopian Women War Veterans: A Feminist Analysis. *Journal of Feminist Family Therapy*, 23(3–4), pp. 163–187. https://doi.org/10.1080/08952833.2011.604536.

O'Connell, A. B. (2016). What Soldiers Do: Sex and the American G.I. in World War II France [review]. *Journal of American History*, 103(1), pp. 152–154.

Oliveira, C. and Baines, E. (2021). "It's Like Giving Birth to This Girl Again": Social Repair and Motherhood after Conflict-Related Sexual Violence. *Social Politics*, 29(2), pp. 750–770. https://doi.org/10.1093/sp/jxab033.

Parkinson, S. E. (2020). Practical Ideology in Militant Organizations. *World Politics*, 73(1), pp. 52–81. https://doi.org/10.1017/s0043887120000180.

Parmelee, J. (1993). Eritrean Women Who Fought in Trenches Now Battle Tradition. *Washington Post* [online], June 25. www.washingtonpost.com/archive/politics/1993/06/25/eritrean-women-who-fought-in-the-trenches-now-battle-tradition/2e4cbbaf-15d7-4fc7-b95a-c66d6b82aad1/.

Parsons, T. R. (2017). All *Askaris* Are Family Men: Sex, Domesticity and Discipline in the King's African Rifles, 1902–1964. In D. Killingray and D. Omissi (eds.), *Guardians of Empire: The Armed Forces of the Colonial Powers c. 1700–1964*. Manchester: Manchester University Press, pp. 157–178. https://doi.org/10.7765/9781526121462.00014.

Parvati, C. (2003). The Question of Women's Leadership in People's War in Nepal. *Problems and Prospects of Revolution in Nepal* [online], www.bannedthought.net/Nepal/Problems-Prospects/w_leadership.html.

Pettigrew, J. and Shneiderman, S. (2004). Women and the Maobaadi: Ideology and Agency in Nepal's Maoist Movement. *Himal Southasian* [online], January 1. www.himalmag.com/ideology-and-agency-in-nepals-maoist-movement/.

Pinaud, C. (2015). "We Are Trained to Be married!": Elite Formation and Ideology in the "Girls' Battalion" of the Sudan People's Liberation Army. *Journal of Eastern African Studies*, 9(3), pp. 375–393. https://doi.org/10.1080/17531055.2015.1091638.

Pomeroy, W. (2011). *The Forest: A Personal Record of the Huk Guerilla Struggle in the Philippines*. Quezon City: University of the Philippines Press.

Reimers, D. M. (1992). *Still the Golden Door: The Third World Comes to America*. New York: Columbia University Press.

Revkin, M. R. and Kao, K. (2020). How Does Punishment Affect Reintegration of Former Offenders? Evidence from Iraq. *SSRN*. https://doi.org/10.2139/ssrn.3659468.

Roblin, S. (2018). The Forgotten Angels of Dien Bien Phu. *War Is Boring* [online]. https://warisboring.com/the-forgotten-angels-of-dien-bien-phu/.

Roy, S. (2006). Revolutionary Marriage: On the Politics of Sexual Stories in Naxalbari. *Feminist Review*, 83(1), pp. 99–118. https://doi.org/10.1057/palgrave.fr.9400283.

Salifu, U., Ndung'u, I., and Sigsworth, R. (2017). Violent Extremism in Kenya: Why Women Are a Priority. *Institute for Security Studies Monographs*, 2017(197) [online]. https://journals.co.za/doi/pdf/10.10520/EJC-b07c07a3e.

Sanín, F. G. and Carranza Franco, F. (2017). Organizing Women for Combat: The Experience of the FARC in the Colombian War. *Journal of Agrarian Change*, 17(4), pp. 770–778. https://doi.org/10.1111/joac.12238.

Schulhofer-Wohl, J. and Sambanis, N. (2020). *Disarmament, Demobilization, and Reintegration Programs: An Assessment*. Stockholm: Folke Bernadotte Academy Publication [online]. https://hdl.handle.net/1887/80556.

Segal, M. W. (1986). The Military and the Family As Greedy Institutions. *Armed Forces and Society*, 13(1), pp. 9–38. https://doi.org/10.1177/0095327x8601300101.

Simpson, C. C. (2002). *An Absent Presence: Japanese Americans in Postwar American Culture, 1945–1960*. Durham, NC: Duke University Press.

Soh, C. S. (2008). *The Comfort Women: Sexual Violence and Postcolonial Memory in Korea and Japan*. Chicago, IL: University of Chicago Press.

Speckhard, A. and Ellenberg, M. (2020). ISIS in Their Own Words: Recruitment History, Motivations for Joining, Travel, Experiences in ISIS, and Disillusionment over Time – Analysis of 220 In-depth Interviews of ISIS Returnees, Defectors and Prisoners. *Journal of Strategic Security*, 13(1), pp. 82–127. https://doi.org/10.5038/1944-0472.13.1.1791.

Spencer, A. (2016). The Hidden Face of Terrorism: An Analysis of the Women in Islamic State. *Journal of Strategic Security*, 9(3), pp. 74–98. https://doi.org/10.5038/1944-0472.9.3.1549.

Stack-O'Connor, A. (2007). Lions, Tigers, and Freedom Birds: How and Why the Liberation Tigers of Tamil Eelam Employs Women. *Terrorism and Political Violence*, 19(1), pp. 43–63. https://doi.org/10.1080/09546550601054642.

Stern, O. and Peterson, C. (2022). *Assisting Women Formerly Associated with al-Shabaab: A Proposed Approach to Programming*. London: Adam Smith International. https://orlystern.com/wp-content/uploads/2023/06/Assisting-women-formerly-assocaited-with-al-Shabaaab.pdf.

Stern, O. M. (2019). *The Invisible Women of Al-Shabaab*. London: Adam Smith International. https://orlystern.com/wp-content/uploads/2023/06/The-Invisible-Women-of-al-Shabaab-.pdf.

Stern, O. M. (2020). *Married in the Shadows: The Wives of al-Shabaab*. London: Adam Smith International. https://orlystern.com/wp-content/uploads/2023/06/Wives-of-al-Shabaab-final.pdf.

Stern, O. M. (2021). *Al-Shabaab's Gendered Economy*. London: Adam Smith International. https://orlystern.com/wp-content/uploads/2023/06/Al-Shabaabs-Gendered-Economy.pdf.

Sthapit, L. and Doneys, P. (2017). Female Maoist Combatants during and after the People's War. In Å. Kolås (ed.), *Women, Peace and Security in Nepal*. New York: Routledge, pp. 33–49.

Suarez, C. and Baines, E. (2021). "Together at the Heart": Familial Relations and the Social Reintegration of Ex-combatants. *International Peacekeeping*, 29(1), pp. 1–23. https://doi.org/10.1080/13533312.2021.1952408.

Swamy, M. R. N. (2003). *Inside an Elusive Mind, Prabhakaran: The First Profile of the World's Most Ruthless Guerrilla Leader.* New Delhi: Konark Publishers.

Tambiah, Y. (2005). Turncoat Bodies: Sexuality and Sex Work under Militarization in Sri Lanka. *Gender and Society*, 19(2), pp. 243–261. https://doi.org/10.1177/0891243204273076.

Teklu, Z. M. (2015). The Women's Movement in Tigray (1976 – Present): Emergence, Development and Relationships with TPLF. MA thesis, University of Bergen.

Thamizhini (2020). *In the Shadow of a Sword: The Memoir of a Woman Leader in the LTTE*. Translated by N. Rodrigo. New Delhi: Sage Publications.

Themnér, A. and Karlén, N. (2020). Building a Safety Net: Explaining the Strength of Ex-military Networks. *Security Studies*, 29(2), pp. 1–33. https://doi.org/10.1080/09636412.2020.1722851.

Trisko Darden, J. and Hassan, D. (2023). Citizenship, Family Law, and the Repatriation of Islamic State Affiliates in MENA. *Terrorism and Political Violence*, pp. 1–15. https://doi.org/10.1080/09546553.2023.2188961.

Trustram, M. (1984). *Women of the Regiment: Marriage and the Victorian Army.* Cambridge: Cambridge University Press.

Upreti, B. R. and Shivakoti, S. (2018). The Struggle of Female Ex-combatants in Nepal. *Peace Review*, 30(1), pp. 78–86. https://doi.org/10.1080/10402659.2017.1419937.

Vale, G. (2019). *Women in Islamic State: From Caliphate to Camps.* International Centre for Counter-Terrorism Policy Brief Report [online]. www.jstor.com/stable/resrep19621.

Van Hook, S. (2012). How Militarism Manipulates the Lives of Women: An Interview with Feminist Scholar Cynthia Enloe. Waging Nonviolence [online], September 13. https://wagingnonviolence.org/2012/09/taking-womens-lives-seriously-an-interview-with-cynthia-enloe/.

Veale, A. (2003). From Child Soldier to Ex-fighter, Female Fighters, Demobilisation and Reintegration in Ethiopia. *Institute for Security Studies Monographs*, 85(2003), pp. 1–69. https://hdl.handle.net/10520/EJC48739.

Veale, A. (2005). Collective and Individual Identities: Experiences of Recruitment and Reintegration of Female Excombatants of the Tigrean People's Liberation Army, Ethiopia. In A. McIntyre (ed.), *Invisible Stakeholders: Children and War in Africa*. Pretoria: Institute of Security Studies (ISS), pp. 105–126 [online]. https://cora.ucc.ie/items/b7b1ec65-3bfc-4ef1-8240-1f920db4e43f.

Voss, B. L. (2008). Domesticating Imperialism: Sexual Politics and the Archaeology of Empire. *American Anthropologist*, 110(2), pp. 191–203. https://doi.org/10.1111/j.1548-1433.2008.00025.x.

Weber, A. (2011). Women without Arms: Gendered Fighter Constructions in Eritrea and Southern Sudan. *International Journal of Conflict and Violence*, 5(2), pp. 357–370. https://doi.org/10.4119/unibi/ijcv.114.

Weinstein, J. M. (2006). *Inside Rebellion: The Politics of Insurgent Violence.* Cambridge University Press.

Winter, C. (2015). *Women of the Islamic State: A Manifesto on Women by the Al-Khanssaa Brigade.* London: Quilliam Foundation.

Wood, E. J. (2003). *Insurgent Collective Action and Civil War in El Salvador.* Cambridge: Cambridge University Press [online]. www.cambridge.org/us/features/wood.

Wood, E. J. (2018). Rape as a Practice of War: Toward a Typology of Political Violence. *Politics and Society*, 46(4), pp. 513–537. https://doi.org/10.1177/0032329218773710.

Yami, H. (2021). *Hisila: From Revolutionary to First Lady.* New York: Penguin Random House.

Zaks, S. (2017). *Resilience beyond Rebellion.* Berkeley: University of California Press.

Zimmerman, S. J. (2020). *Militarizing Marriage: West African Soldiers' Conjugal Traditions in Modern French Empire.* Athens: Ohio University Press.

Acknowledgments

I am grateful to many people for their helpful comments, feedback, and encouragement in the process of crafting this Element. I extend my heartfelt thanks to the participants in Elisabeth Wood's advisee working group at Yale, to Libby herself for her guidance as an advisor and mentor, to the participants at the Workshop on Under-Researched Aspects of Gender and Security at the University of Amsterdam, to the attendees of my guest lectures at the University of Amsterdam and Princeton University where I presented drafts of this work, as well as to Sarah Zimmerman, Meredith Loken, and Meg Guliford for their comments on early drafts. I also extend my gratitude to Ana Julia Rodrigues Alves for all her help formatting this Element.

Furthermore, I am exceptionally appreciative of the guidance of this series' editors, Tiffany D. Barnes and Diana Z. O'Brien, for their encouragement and assistance throughout the process. I am also grateful to the two anonymous reviewers for their helpful comments. I am eternally appreciative of the men and women in Ethiopia who took the time to speak with me as I conducted fieldwork for my dissertation, which eventually led me to this Element.

Finally, I am profoundly lucky to have an unfailingly supportive family. To my parents: thank you for your exuberance and unconditional love. Thanks for teaching me that there is no problem too big to make a joke out of or a grievance too small to call you about. To Dan: thank you for being my personal barista, training partner, and best friend. Being married to you is one of the most fun and fulfilling experiences of my life, but don't tell anybody.

To my parents, for showing me what a good marriage looks like; to Dan, for choosing us every day; and to Miriam and Fikru for sharing their story.

Cambridge Elements $\equiv$

Gender and Politics

Tiffany D. Barnes
University of Kentucky

Tiffany D. Barnes is Professor of Political Science at the University of Kentucky. She is the author of *Women, Politics, and Power: A Global Perspective* (Rowman & Littlefield, 2007) and the award-winning *Gendering Legislative Behavior* (Cambridge University Press, 2016). Her research has been funded by the National Science Foundation (NSF) and recognized with numerous awards. Barnes is the former president of the Midwest Women's Caucus and the founder and director of the Empirical Study of Gender (EGEN) network.

Diana Z. O'Brien
Washington University in St. Louis

Diana Z. O'Brien is the Bela Kornitzer Distinguished Professor of Political Science at Washington University in St. Louis. She specializes in the causes and consequences of women's political representation. Her award-winning research has been supported by the NSF and published in leading political science journals. O'Brien has also served as a Fulbright Visiting Professor, an associate editor at *Politics & Gender*, the president of the Midwest Women's Caucus, and a founding member of the EGEN network.

About the Series

From campaigns and elections to policymaking and political conflict, gender pervades every facet of politics. Elements in Gender and Politics features carefully theorized, empirically rigorous scholarship on gender and politics. The Elements both offer new perspectives on foundational questions in the field and identify and address emerging research areas.

Cambridge Elements ☰

Gender and Politics

Elements in the Series

In Love and at War: Marriage in Non-state Armed Groups
Hilary Matfess

A full series listing is available at: www.cambridge.org/EGAP

Milton Keynes UK
Ingram Content Group UK Ltd.
UKHW010729050224
437294UK00020B/977